#PEACE

A NEW PERSPECTIVE OF HOPE:
A BEAUTIFUL COMPILATION ABOUT THE THREE
ASPECTS OF PEACE

Compiled by: Anita Sechesky

LWL PUBLISHING HOUSE
Brampton, Canada

#Peace – A New Perspective of Hope: A Beautiful Compilation about the Three Aspects of Peace
Copyright © 2016 by LWL PUBLISHING HOUSE
A division of Anita Sechesky – Living Without Limitations Inc.

All rights reserved. No part of this publication may be reproduced, distributed or transmitted in any form or by any means, including photocopying, recording, or other electronic or mechanical methods, without prior written permission of the publisher, except in the case of brief quotations embodied in critical reviews and certain other noncommercial uses permitted by copyright law. For permission requests, write to the publisher, addressed "Attention: Permissions Coordinator," at the address below.

Anita Sechesky – Living Without Limitations Inc.
asechesky@hotmail.ca
lwlclienthelp@gmail.com
www.lwlpublishinghouse.com

Publisher's Note: This book is a collection of personal experiences written at the discretion of each co-author. LWL PUBLISHING HOUSE uses American English spelling as its standard. Each co-author's word usage and sentence structure have remained unaltered as much as possible to retain the authenticity of each chapter.

Book Layout © 2016 LWL PUBLISHING HOUSE

#Peace – A New Perspective of Hope: A Beautiful Compilation about the Three Aspects of Peace
Anita Sechesky – Living Without Limitations Inc.
ISBN 978-0-9939648-5-5
ASIN 0993964855

Book Cover: LWL PUBLISHING HOUSE
Inside Layout: LWL PUBLISHING HOUSE

CONTENTS

LEGAL DISCLAIMER 1

FOREWORD 3

ACKNOWLEDGMENTS 7

DEDICATION 9

INTRODUCTION 11

CHAPTER ONE 19
   Peace is Personal
   By Anita Sechesky

PEACEFUL POINT 23
   #Peace is Found in the Heart
   By Darla Ouellette

CHAPTER TWO 25
   Peace Will Give You Silence and Beauty Within
   By Chadi Hemaidan

PEACEFUL POINT 29
   #Peace Through My Personal Perspective
   By Tim Rahija

CHAPTER THREE 31
   The Missing Peace
   By Steve Yuzenko

PEACEFUL POINT 35
   #Peace is How You Make It
   By Marigrace Galura

CHAPTER FOUR 37
   Peace and Tranquility is Still Possible
   By Elani Kay

CHAPTER FIVE ...39
Peaceful Perceptions from Pain Are Still Possible
By Elizabeth Ann Pennington

PEACEFUL POINT ...45
#Peace is the Love of My Child
By Malini Siva

CHAPTER SIX ...47
Five Habits to Finding Inner Peace
By Pamela Kunopaskie

PEACEFUL POINT ...53
#Peace is Pampering Yourself
By Sabinah Adewole

CHAPTER SEVEN ...55
Recognizing Peace in the Lowest of Places
By Stephanie Roy

PEACEFUL POINT ...59
#Peace and Individuality
By Jossine Abrahams

CHAPTER EIGHT ...61
Finding My Peace through Faith and Fear
By Karlene Johnson

CHAPTER NINE ...67
Peace is Powerful
By Anita Sechesky

CHAPTER TEN ...69
A Silent and Peaceful Connection
By Kathie Tuhkanen

PEACEFUL POINT ...73
#Peace is a Name to Live "Up To"
By Mary Hilty

CHAPTER ELEVEN 75
Surviving Life's Losses with the Peace of God
By Leah Lucas

CHAPTER TWELVE 81
Reflections of Peace through the Years
By Ruth Farvardin

PEACEFUL POINT 85
#Peace is Being Present
By Marigrace Galura

CHAPTER THIRTEEN 87
Let Your Peace Shine
By Darla Ouellette

PEACEFUL POINT 91
#Peace, Perfect Peace
By Jossine Abrahams

CHAPTER FOURTEEN 93
In Search of My Peaceful Connection
By Susan Kern

CHAPTER FIFTEEN 99
Life's Pressures Bring out Our Perfect Peace
By Randall Mitchell

PEACEFUL POINT 103
#Peace is Personally Manifested
By Marie Woods

CHAPTER SIXTEEN 107
Overcoming Human Nature to Find Peace
By Troy Smith

PEACEFUL POINT 111
#Peace is You and Me
By Diana Alli D'souza

CHAPTER SEVENTEEN 113
  Finding the Pathway to My Peace
  By Mary Hilty

CHAPTER EIGHTEEN 119
  Peace is Perfected
  By Anita Sechesky

CHAPTER NINETEEN 123
  Creating the Ultimate Life of Peace
  By Tim Rahija

PEACEFUL POINT 127
  #Peace within Prayer
  By Darla Ouellette

CHAPTER TWENTY 129
  Life Seasons of Peace
  By Candace Hawkshaw

CHAPTER TWENTY-ONE 133
  Get in Touch with Your Soul to Save Our Planet
  By Janine Moore

PEACEFUL POINT 137
  #Peace for the Mind of a Single Mom
  By Kathie Tuhkanen

CHAPTER TWENTY-TWO 139
  Raising Vibrations to Find Your Inner Peace
  By Jewels Rafter

PEACEFUL POINT 147
  #Peace is Within Your Heart's Home
  By Laura Haskell

CHAPTER TWENTY-THREE 149
  Divine Peace, Love and Healing
  By Susan Mantz

PEACEFUL POINT 153
#Peace – Humanity's Journey
By Troy Smith

CHAPTER TWENTY-FOUR 155
Peace – Touch Me Like the Feather of a Dove
By Diana Alli D'souza

PEACEFUL POINT 159
#Peace and Persistence
By Mary Hilty

CHAPTER TWENTY-FIVE 161
The Journey to Peace Through Transformation
By Jennifer Martel

PEACEFUL POINT 167
#Peace Through the Seasons
By Anna Jacono Paveling

CHAPTER TWENTY-SIX 169
Healed By a Hug
By Sandi Chomyn

CHAPTER TWENTY-SEVEN 173
Peaceful Spirit
By Anita Sechesky

CHAPTER TWENTY-EIGHT 177
Peace Always Attracts Love
By Anita Sechesky

CHAPTER TWENTY-NINE 181
Discovering Peace in Your Life
By Anita Sechesky

CONCLUSION 185

LEGAL DISCLAIMER

The information and content contained within this book *#Peace – A New Perspective of Hope: A Beautiful Compilation about the Three Aspect of Peace* does not substitute any form of professional counsel such as a Psychologist, Physician, Life Coach, or Counselor. The contents and information provided does not constitute professional or legal advice in any way, shape or form.

All chapters are written at the discretion of and with the full accountability of each writer. Anita Sechesky – Living Without Limitations Inc. or LWL PUBLISHING HOUSE is not liable or responsible for any of the specific details, descriptions of people, places or things, personal interpretations, stories and experiences contained within. The Publisher is not liable for any misrepresentations, false or unknown statements, actions, or judgments made by any of the contributors or their chapter contents in this book. Each contributor is responsible for their own submissions and have shared their stories in good faith to encourage others.

Any decisions you make and the outcomes thereof are entirely your own doing. Under no circumstances can you hold the Compiler, LWL PUBLISHING HOUSE, or "Anita Sechesky – Living Without Limitations Inc." liable for any actions that you take.

You agree not to hold the Compiler, LWL PUBLISHING HOUSE, or "Anita Sechesky – Living Without Limitations Inc." liable for any loss or expense incurred by you, as a result of materials, advice, coaching or mentoring offered within.

The information offered in this book is intended to be general information with respect to general life issues. Information is offered in good faith; however, you are under no obligation to use this information.

Nothing contained in this book shall be considered legal, financial, or actuarial advice.

The author or Publisher assume no liability or responsibility to actual events or stories being portrayed.

It may introduce what a Life Coach, Counselor or Therapist may discuss with you at any given time during scheduled sessions. The advice contained herein is not meant to replace the Professional roles of a physician or any of these professions.

FOREWORD

Peace. The final frontier of emotional health. Inner peace is what we strive for when we enter the therapy context so that we can actually have a good quality of life. Living without peace is like being a frog put in a pot of cold water atop a hot stove that is unknowingly slowly boiling to death. The frog sits there quite unaware of its fate since it keeps adjusting to the temperature, not fully realizing the impending doom that awaits it. Like the adaptable frog in water, we tend to normalize chaos if that is what we grew up with.

When I think about having inner peace, I think of having the emotional freedom from the enslaving emotions of fear, guilt, shame, and rage. These emotions are learned and metabolized as normal often in family-cultures that are dysfunctional. From these, a person is forced to develop a "false self" as a way of surviving and coping. There are many versions of what the false self may be, but all of them contribute to robbing a person of inner peace. For example (and this is just one example), the family-culture might have taught that it's important to please everybody; placing the self-care instinct way down on the totem pole of priorities. Pleasing everyone else becomes the "disease-to-please" as an instinctual way of being and all boundary setting impulses give way to a kind of robot-like obligation feeling to meet everyone else's needs over your own. However, when a person lives and operates from the disease-to-please, I observe that the pattern lands the person feeling deep resentment and depression as well as profound lack of inner peace.

There is plenty of evidence showing that living in a constant state of emotional turmoil that is, in a constant state of lack of inner peace, will compromise a person's immune system as well as their mental health. As a psychotherapist with a holistic sensibility, in private practice since the early '90's, I observe that people living without a sense of inner peace or without a road map to get there are robbed of hope, trust, and faith which deteriorates their resilience to life's turmoil and tough lessons. They come at life ungrounded and out of touch with what truly makes them happy and peaceful.

I also notice that urban modern living has promoted a type of addiction to activity, chaos, achievement, and yes there is that media vetted glorification of drama! For a person to find their inner peace, they need to actually go about the process of dismantling their overly enmeshed relationship to busyness, chaos, future worrying, and past obsessing and this requires lots of practice and inner discipline. This is the only way to rewire the deep neural pathways associated with that old way of being. Many tell me that living in a peaceful state is so foreign to them that they literally begin feeling an overwhelming sensation of boredom, fear, unease, and sometimes even depression and anxiety when their life becomes peaceful. It is not uncommon for a client to look at me with a horrified and annoyed expression as I introduce simple mindful slow breathing exercises. Many are also very impacted by their inner FOMO (Fear of Missing Out) battle cry as they begin the journey toward balance and peace!

Yet the road to true joy and happiness begins with having more inner peace. To that end I encourage my clients and readers to deeply observe their pattern of constantly looking for the next shiny thing to keep them stimulated or the next "other person's" problem to keep them in chaos. These are major avoidance tactics from actually dealing with the self.

What I have observed is that finding inner peace involves the pursuit of your self-culture. This is your authentic, instinctive self that brings on a deep sense of self-knowing, self-care, and a habit of filling your own cup first and giving to others only from the overflow. Having self-culture brings on a deep self-compassion and self-acceptance. Through this you are able to breakdown resentment, anger, shame, and all the emotional afflictions that rob you of peace. You are also doing your part to stop multi-generational dysfunction dead in its tracks. And let me emphasize, self-culture and inner peace do not come without drawing gentle but clear boundaries, which requires that you know what is okay for you and what is not. This is also the road to peaceful relationships with others. In fact, I think the kindest, most compassionate, and peaceful people are those that are in touch with what is okay for them and what is not.

The true and profound richness of life begins when you stop long enough to slow your breathing down so you can experience a "felt" sense of peacefulness which then makes your deep, inner, authentic voice (your self-culture) louder in your mind than all other voices in the mix.

The planet needs the real you, and it is time that you began that journey! The pursuit of self-culture is a hard one for many of us in the face of what we may have learned from our family-cultures, and I have unlimited compassion for those who embark on this path. I want to emphasize that the quest for your self-culture is not a narcissistic, selfish, futile, self-indulgent pursuit. It is vital to your well-being as well as the planet's, due to the peace that emerges from that pursuit. You can only serve those you love and the planet better when you know who you are and are at peace with yourself.

The journey to peace is a profound, and at times arduous, look within.

The result will be an emerging self that you will treasure, savor, and protect and the planet will gain a being that is loving, compassionate, and generous. These are the elixirs for true peace and the alchemy to maintain ongoing peace.

Let me just say how honored and delighted I was to be asked to write the forward to this book by the incomparable Anita Sechesky who is a tireless agent for positivity and living without limitations! She is a warm soul and a deep thinker. This book bravely explores the concept of peace through the viewpoint of thirty voices from all over the world! The writers reveal deep stories that bring to light both personal and global journeys with respect to peace. This book is sure to make an impact on our beloved planet which is in profound need of healing. I feel blessed to be able participate in this positive project! May peace prevail.

Victoria Lorient-Faibish MEd, RP, CCC, BCPP, RPE is a Registered Psychotherapist, relationship expert, life coach, author and keynote speaker. For twenty years, she has witnessed the metamorphosis of countless people as they journey toward their "self-culture" and their healthy "relationship-cultures." She has studied energy psychology modalities and her influences include Buddhism, Reiki, osteopathy, visualization, meditation, as well as modern and traditional psychotherapy; the basis for her brand of holistic psychotherapy that works with the mind, body, and soul to effect monumental change in her clients' lives.

Her first book, "Find Your "Self-Culture": Moving from Depression and Anxiety to Monumental Self-Acceptance" offers a way out of the rabbit hole of depression and anxiety through profound awareness, self-love, and acceptance.

Her second book, "Connecting: Rewire Your Relationship-Culture" teaches readers how to use brain science to heal multi-generational relationship dysfunction.

Dini Petty wrote the forward to the book and says: "This book would have made my journey shorter and easier. It will guide you through your family matrix, into dating in the modern world, how to spot relationship dysfunction from the start, and finally lead you into healthy relationships and enduring marriages."

Victoria Lorient-Faibish MEd, RP, CCC, BCPP, RPE
Registered Psychotherapist
Relationship Expert
Holistic Psychotherapist
Masters in Educational Psychology
Canadian Certified Counsellor
Board Certified Polarity Practitioner
Registered Polarity Educator
Website: http://www.visualizationworks.com
YouTube Channel: http://www.youtube.com/askvictoria

ACKNOWLEDGMENTS

It is with sincere appreciation and gratitude that I take this time to acknowledge the people who have stood by, supported, and loved me for exactly who I am. Through all things I am blessed because of the peace of God and the blanket of love that continually surrounds me and lifts me up.

Thank you Stephen, the love of my life for believing in me and my desire to always strive for greater purpose in all that I do. Your unconditional love, support, and friendship has inspired me on this journey. Thank you for helping me to establish LWL PUBLISHING HOUSE and standing by me and my vision to make this dream come true.

To my eldest son Nathaniel: Thank you for being a such a wise and inspiring young man. I'm so proud of you and your accomplishments. I thank God for you and how you are growing into a such a brilliant and responsible young man. You inspire me daily. Never let anyone tell you that you cannot become the best you possible. You were a success from the day you were born. You are perfect to me and I will always believe in you. Love Mom.

To Sammy: Thank you, my darling son, for the joy that you bring to all of us. You never cease to amaze me with your growing wisdom and skills. God has great plans for you. You are perfect to me. Success is in every step that you take. I'm so proud to call you "My little darling". I will always believe in you. Love Mommy.

To my beautiful and loving Mom, Jean Seergobin: Thank you so much for always encouraging me to never give up in life, I love you so much with all my heart. It is because of you that I have learned to be strong and still have compassion for others. Whenever I needed a friend, you've always been there for me. Thank you Mom for everything that you do.

To my Dad, Jetty Seergobin: Thank you for teaching me to reach for higher goals in life, and to carry on despite whatever circumstances I may be facing. Mom and Dad, I love you both so much because of your unconditional and unfailing love for me. You have both encouraged, inspired, motivated, and blessed me in so many ways that have contributed to the successful person I have become today. I am ever so thankful for your love and prayers over my life. It is because of your love and support towards me that I am inspired and encouraged to dream, do more for others, and still grow emotionally stronger through my own experiences. I pray blessings of health, wholeness, happiness, and longevity over both of you. May the grace of God's divine love and protection be always around you. I love you Mom and Dad.

To my brother Trevor Seergobin: Thank you for believing in me and encouraging me to never give up on my dreams no matter who was part of my life or not. Your continued love, support, and motivation has always been a blessing to me.

I would like to give a special thanks of appreciation to Victoria Lorient-Faibish for writing the Foreword for our book. Her beautiful energy and insightful wisdom has added so much value for our readers to understand that there are resources available, should they be required.

Thank you to my amazing co-authors. Each and every one of you contributed to making our book a work of art. Your perspectives will forever enlighten and inspire so many souls to believe that peace is possible.

For all of the people who have been part of my life, supported my dreams and ambitions, thank you for always believing in me. I love and appreciate each and every one of you. I am grateful to every individual who has contributed to the woman that I am today. Yet, there were many seasonal friendships that have come along side for a short time and for that I acknowledge and appreciate you for sharing that moment of your life with me. I have not forgotten. You are always in a special place within my heart.

Once again I would like to give an unusual appreciation to those who have caused me heartache, disappointments, and pain. You were the lessons that I needed at that time in my life so that I am a better person today. Because of you, I will never give up in life. It was the hardships that you caused me, which made me strive more to believe in forgiveness, peace, and love that is lacking in this world. Two wrongs never make a right. I forgive.

Love always covers a multitude of sins. ~ 1 Peter 4:8

DEDICATION

This book is dedicated to everyone, especially the grandparents, parents, and their children, who understand the true meaning of peace and will carry it through to the next generation. Peace is a personal experience that begins at home. Peace is powerful when it is shared between others. Peace is perfected as we apply it to every experience in our lives.

Anita Sechesky

INTRODUCTION

I'm so blessed to be the main Author, Visionary, Compiler, and the Publisher of this beautiful book which is already connected to a family of Best-Selling publications. My very first book in the #Hashtag series, *"#Love – A New Generation of Hope"* (1st edition), became a #1 International Best-Seller on Amazon.ca, within a few short hours on November 24th, 2014, the day it was officially launched online. Then on December 4th, 2015, my company, LWL PUBLISHING HOUSE, relaunched a revised edition of that beautiful book entitled *"#Love – A New Generation of Hope Continues..."* with 22 additional Love Notes sprinkled throughout the book. It hit #2 International Best-Seller on launch day, and #1 Hot New Release, once again.

The #Hashtag series of books is an exciting line of creative and unique books bringing enlightened individuals from all over the globe the opportunity to join into a collaboration with our successfully established publishing team of like-minded and caring individuals, together creating a healing wave of inspiration and empowerment in every life we touch. This book was birthed from my vision of helping to create an awareness that Peace is one of the most instrumental behaviors that is actually an action, energy, and emotion that human beings are all capable of creating within their lives and around their environment. It's the invisible thread that's created when little children happily play together and is powerful enough to unite nations and change the world if we can truly see how significant it really is.

Pulling from all my professional training and practices as a Registered Nurse, Certified Professional Coach, Best-Seller Publisher, and Book writing Coach, along with my creative and highly energetic marketing and media skills, I utilize them effectively because I love to empower and promote all my clients. The primary intention of this book series for me, a successful author and Publisher, is for each one of my books to release a global shift of hope and healing into our beautiful but hurting world. I would like to take this moment and welcome you, our beloved readers, as we embrace the magnitude of what it takes to manifest a peaceful life and all its benefits, not just for us but for those around us. So without further delay let's talk about #Peace and what kind of possibilities can be created from living a life without limitations, which allows us to experience the most serene, productive, and healthy way of living.

Peace is a powerful emotion that cannot be seen, but yet it can be felt within the human spirit. We can notice the calming and cohesive effects it creates between two otherwise opposing individuals. The topic of #Peace is something many people freely think and wonder about. Yet, in a sense it's so expensive can cost you the most valuable relationships that were meant to last a lifetime. However, it remains without any known monetary value. Peace is highly personable and easy to maintain in one's life, if you choose to follow its few basic and simplistic rules. For instance, do you allow things to fester and get out of control when triggered by another emotional reaction or response? It's a subject that's dear to my heart and soul as I strongly feel Peace is something so many of us can misunderstand and forget about. I highly regard it as one of the most important things in our lives. The very nature in making a statement like this may seem simplistic and well-intended, but I reassure you that after reading the forty chapters of this book, ranging in length from 300 to 3000 words, I'm beyond blessed at the reveal of this book and how it has unfolded even better than I could have perceived. Our gorgeous cover depicts the level of tranquility and stillness our readers will experience as they step into the realm of peaceful solutions and abilities to apply from the hearts and souls of all thirty contributors.

I believe Peace is so powerful because, next to love, it's the same thing we all desire, and is the common goal that every man, woman, and child needs as a cornerstone to a healthy and productive life. Peace can bring adversaries together and create an accord where it never existed. Peace is silent but yet strong enough to create an atmosphere of love, healing, and unity.

I have centered this Anthology on three specific themes which I have identified as the most enlightening aspects of Peace sensed by everyone, whether or not they are consciously aware of it. No matter who and where we are in life, we are all equal and it can be observed through the loving relationships we have at any given time. I strongly believe that we are always exposed to at least two, if not all three of these perspectives of Peace. I decided to break down what peace is on a personal scale, and how it affects so many levels of our well-being. We then delve into how powerful peace can be in our daily lives and the interactions around us. Lastly, our third theme focuses on how our lives are perfected by this amazing quality. We carry emotional attachments to the people, places, and things that we all experience on a personal level. The very act of existing in this world itself is a powerful medium which allows us to form cherished and deep relationships with many individuals.

This book was beautifully created from the heart strings of each one of my thirty contributors, who decided they wanted to be part of something bigger than themselves. The stories and memories are meant to touch your very soul. It doesn't matter who you are or where you come from, your life is one that needs peace to maintain health and well-being.

The stories in this book are aligned to the vision that God placed into my heart at a very young age. I knew what it felt like to be the one who didn't fit in. I was different in my physical appearance as my family immigrated to Canada from Guyana, South America when I was just a young child at the sweet age of four. My skin tone reflected the beautiful golden hue from being born a warm, lush, and tropical country. There, I had already been introduced into Nursery School system with great friends. I was accepted and loved for who I was! I remember going out when it rained tropical buckets – there were huge mud puddles to jump in afterwards. My once playful and carefree life was instantly transformed as we relocated to Northwestern Ontario. I had to learn a whole new way of adapting into a society that was in the middle of a winter deep freeze with temperatures ranging from minus 25 to minus 40 below. Yes, it was a very brutal cultural shock for all of us. Not only was the climate cold, we soon discovered that the citizens in this part of the world were not the warmest at times either.

So you see, my vision for *#Peace – A New Perspective of Hope* is something that has always been a part of who I am as a person. When I grew up, I trained to be a Registered Nurse who cares for all peoples regardless of race, color, religion (creed), gender, age, national origin, or disability. There is no discrimination in health care as there should be none in all the other areas of our lives.

I learned tolerance at an early age. My life training involved understanding that a huge part of acceptance towards others encompassed searching your own heart to understand that people are always going to respond based on how they are feeling and what their personal experiences are. Who am I to judge? My parents are my heroes in every sense of the word. They have taught me to accept people who would never accept me and to forgive others who would never forgive me. You see, life is all about choices. Love and peace are unlimited because they come from God, whose profound peace is unlimited towards us. The more love you give the more you get back. It may not come from where you imagine but it always does come back to find you and lift you up when you least expect.

Every one of the passages within this book come from perspectives that are quite incredible when you really begin to comprehend that each person we encounter is on a journey of discovering who they are also. We are all connected some way by our energies and ultimately in a spiritual sense. I have invited each of my contributing writers to search deeply within their hearts and souls, permitting themselves to safely bare their emotions about where they once were and compare it to where they are today. Peace is an energy as much as an emotion to practice. It always surprises me how the human spirit is so strong and resilient to endure the things we face but not always brave enough to talk about without possibly feeling shame, embarrassment, or fear of ridicule.

Personally, my faith is what has brought me through so many things as well as the love and knowledge that I have very precious people in my life who love and appreciate me for who I am. Many times, people do not realize that the reason they are struggling is due to the love and peace that is missing somewhere in their emotional make-up, whether it is from a parent, child, spouse, relative, or friend. Living a peaceful life is what links all of our positive interactions.

For those who are still lacking peace in their lives, cannot find a way to heal the emptiness, and have become so discouraged, my message for you is never give up! Continue peacefully on your voyage and allow yourself the time to forgive those who have damaged this precious quality within you. You can still appreciate that there is a world of like-minded individuals waiting to embrace you in warmth and acceptance. Peace is always within you. Give it the chance to grow once more.

Anita Sechesky is a Best-Seller Publisher, Registered Nurse, Certified Professional Coach, NLP and LOA Wealth Practitioner, Best-Seller Consultant, multiple International Best-Selling Author, as well as a Workshop Facilitator and Conference Host. She is the Founder and CEO of Anita Sechesky - Living Without Limitations Inc. and the Founder and Publisher of LWL PUBLISHING HOUSE. Anita was born in Guyana, South America and moved to Canada when she was only four years old. Assisting many people to break through their own limiting beliefs in life and business, Anita had discovered her passion to help individuals release their stories into successful publications. She has five Best-Selling books, including four anthologies, in which approximately 200 International authors and co-authors have benefited to date from her expertise. Anita launched her first solo book *"Absolutely You – Overcome False Limitations and Reach Your Full Potential"* in November 2014. As a Best-Seller Publisher, Anita helps people to put their positive perspectives into print.

Currently, we are looking for co-authors for all of our #Hashtag books in the series and more…

#Hope – A New Way to Think

#Joy – The Emotion to Embrace

#Success - Found within Me

To begin the exciting journey as a VIP Compiler™ with Anita on your own anthology book, or to learn more about becoming a co-author with LWL PUBLISHING HOUSE in one of our many anthologies.

Join my Private Facebook group: LIVING WITHOUT LIMITATIONS LIFESTYLE – With exclusive prizes, co-authoring opportunities and Random Contests with FREE Publishing opportunities. *Empowerment Webinar classes and more - http://bit.ly/1TlsTSm

Book Facebook Fan page: http://bit.ly/211XffM
Facebook: s://www.facebook.com/AnitaSechesky/
Email: lwlclienthelp@gmail.com
YouTube Channel: http://bit.ly/1VEGHew
Website: www.anitasechesky.com
LinkedIn: https://ca.linkedin.com/in/asechesky
Twitter: https://twitter.com/nursie4

PEACE IS PERSONAL

CHAPTER ONE by Anita Sechesky

Peace is Personal

In order for an individual to acquire a true nature of peace for self – from a heart of love and gratitude, there must be a divine connection to your source, whatever you may perceive that to be. We all come from somewhere outside of who we are in our physical state of being. For some people, this means a divine connection to our Creator and God of the universe. Eventually, we must strive to understand that no matter what we are going through, our lives are still connected so that what we feel, think, or perceive may be affected by our actions and attitudes towards any given situation at any moment.

We must positively develop into people who choose to understand and appreciate one another. As we journey inside our hearts and souls, we discover a desire pulling us into a mindful state of constant gratitude, safety, and happiness. We might still find ourselves in moments of unpleasant emotions disrupting our inner calmness and security. It's not an easy journey as many will admit because there will be times of confusion and unbalance. As confident as we appear, we can still become our worst critic and many times the limitations and perceptions that we hold on to are based upon the most unique, disturbing experiences affecting us during times of weakness and vulnerability.

As individuals of reaction and response, our behaviors are based on the things that we are constantly exposed to. They say habits are easily formed by the unconscious and selective process of who we are choosing to be associated with. Many times, if we don't pay attention to these choices, we mirror the behaviors and actions of these very people. It's not always easy to separate ourselves from individuals we have gotten comfortable being around, regardless of the nature of the connection. Because of this, many will continue to stay in damaging relationships, refusing to step outside of their associations. When this happens, we are left in a stagnated growth emotionally and mentally, all the while life keeps on going. We continue to age and mature as our appearance changes, but our emotional well-being is slowly damaged. Sadly, we allow so many of our life decisions to fall into a familiar pattern of safety. The potential within us is deeply scarred and languishing because we have not allowed ourselves the proper amount of introspective observation to gain peace and solitude with those painful situations. We become limited in our lives. The peace that should be there to bring in the confidence and well-being is constantly overshadowed and cannot shine into the greatest light it can possibly become.

In order for there to be real change and healing, we must often choose the act of forgiveness as the positive channel to release all of our negative and pent up energy that can eventually decay the inside of us. By allowing these new and positive thoughts to heal our damaged emotions, we are shifting the energy around us to that of more peace and gratitude. You see, unforgiveness, anger, hate, and all its negative behaviors are of low vibration and cannot produce anything good as a result. Sadly, this is still misunderstood and many people are not aware of why they may have a false sense of peaceful tranquility. You see, if one strives for a healthy and confident mindset, all negative attitudes and behaviors must be addressed and determined by what kind of attachments have actually been permitted into one's life. So many times, you will see individuals who attest to having the ultimate achievement we all desire, that of inner harmony and satisfaction, magnified by the power of love, financial security, and social contentment. They want you to believe they've arrived. It's up to you to determine what you see and what they want you to see. Every single person must interact and grow from relationships with others. There's just no way you can avoid this human experience. As we become more connected with those outside our inner circle, we then start to examine ourselves differently, as every connection brings its own set of experiences, for example, more setbacks, failures, challenges, disappointments, and opportunities to grow and develop into our best self yet. Whatever the event, life will always present us many chances to change our responses. The choice to be at peace, despite everything, is ours to make.

When we come to understand that being centered is when the heart is at peace, our divine connection to God of our universe becomes a confidence that is unwavering and reassures us in times of uncertainty that we can get through just about anything if we believe in ourselves and something bigger than we can conceive. For someone to achieve this state of gratitude, they must understand that life is a story that they get to co-create. Our emotional state is created by our reality, based on our attachment to the outcome, so when seeking a peaceful experience in life, we must comprehend that there is a requirement of us to also put effort into developing the miracle of peace, through mediation, forgiveness, prayer or acceptance of a situation. Often times we find ourselves in situations where we cannot get into a meditative or calming state and there is so much happening around us, we simply cannot achieve the balance and stability we are in need of to not be personally affected by our environment. It's at these moments that a trained mind will follow the rules of grounding yourself into a place of security.

We can do this through visualization and prayer or a positive affirmation will work as well. Most people choose to associate miracles and positive outcomes to the understanding that they have deposited a portion of faith, moral thoughts, and optimistic attitudes towards their anticipated outcome. Many times, life's painful experiences are the contributing factors causing people to demand within themselves that which makes them invincible.

Throughout life's journey, the human spirit perseveres through many difficulties that would have otherwise taken us down had we not had an ounce of peace that prevails. As we are pulled in many directions, we establish patterns of emotional perceptions based on many factors. The following stories throughout this book touch on these such things of great magnitude. For instance, developing and seeking a life of peace and gratitude commences in early childhood and is most often influenced by the content we are exposed to from other human behaviors regardless of who they are and where they fit into our lives, both negative and positive. It will impact the very essence of that person who experiences these situations to determine what level of peace do they have in their lives at that moment and do they want to maintain it regardless of whatever it takes. These experiences may include the loss of a loved one, having to face life-threatening conditions, a devastating diagnosis, traumatic and abusive relationships, family rifts, as well as other moments not fondly recalled. As we choose to remember, many times what happens may not be directly associated to who you are, but life will always give you experiences aligned to the vibrational energy of those you are closely connected with. Once you keep in mind that you might even be a receiver from the energies of those you are not even associated with any longer. The very nature that you have interacted with someone at any given point, vibrationally sets you up for some kind of universal reminder of that person. That's why we must diligently strive to develop a peaceful oasis that emanates from within, as responsible beings come to recognize and appreciate how magnificent a gift it really is to rediscover our confidence in our peaceful mindset and emotional intelligence is the reason we have the ability to gain this ownership of our lives despite what circumstances we face in our daily lives.

By understanding that your life has equal value, just as those you are connected with, allows your higher self to appreciate and connect with others on a more authentic and sincere level. This is a huge deal for those who have suffered from neglect or abusive and traumatic experiences where they were vulnerable enough to allow the situation to hurt them deeply. Although this may have happened unexpectedly, it does not mean it was the victim's fault in any way, shape, or form. It just means that the awareness of the pain has actually strengthened the individual enough to shift them from a victim mentality to self-empowerment and strong enough to maintain a level of peace and healing through various steps possibly involving forgiveness, not only of the individual who inflicted the wrong, but an acceptance to forgive one's self for being in the situation to begin with.

A heart of peace and gratitude is beautifully cultured from deep reflective and often times the most life-altering experiences. People will carry on doing the same things repetitively, supposing a changed outcome each time, and still not have the peace they are seeking after. Regrettably, they don't identify that the resolution is familiarizing themselves to a whole new perspective that unlocks windows of opportunities, allowing them the ability to heal, evolve and effortlessly grow. I often wonder about how it would impact the lives of those who feel trapped and isolated, that nothing is impossible if they choose to be understanding and abundance mindset to appreciate that in order to love the life they have been blessed with, they must develop a continual process of forgiveness and love allowing the peace to be recognized in their interactions with others in their lives. Releasing the baggage and sadness resulting from the unforgiveness and pain will allow the stagnant negative energy and low vibrations to be released from their energetic physiology. As they choose to make an effort in their thought processes, emotional intelligence, verbal and emotional triggers, as well as the behavioral reactions towards everyone around them, the vibrations remain positive and higher positive energy from the power of love envelopes the peaceful aura around and through them creating a simple but significant change in thoughts, actions and external attitudes. Once we choose to continue attracting more positive and peaceful experiences and it will begin healing our very souls.

Examining my own life, I have also experienced the struggle to hold my peace when I had no control over the outcome based on actions of the other individual involved. I learned that if there are unsettled events in my life, there will always directly be some sort of disruption and blockage of peaceful blessings and gratitude. This is what permits a renewal of perspectives to create a life shift in future viewpoints and it's results.

Peace is personal, but it still recognizes that it is contingent on the interactions of all people you are connected with. However, it is one of the most satisfying voyages you step into. May your journeys be peaceful.

Anita Sechesky is a Best-Seller Publisher, Registered Nurse, Certified Professional Coach, NLP and LOA Wealth Practitioner, Best-Seller Consultant, multiple International Best-Selling Author, as well as a Workshop Facilitator and Conference Host. She is the Founder and CEO of Anita Sechesky - Living Without Limitations Inc. and the Founder and Publisher of LWL PUBLISHING HOUSE. Anita was born in Guyana, South America and moved to Canada when she was only four years old. Assisting many people to break through their own limiting beliefs in life and business, Anita had discovered her passion to help individuals release their stories in-to successful publications. She has five Best-Selling books, including four anthologies, in which approximately 200 International authors and co-authors have benefited to date from her expertise. Anita launched her first solo book "Absolutely You – Overcome False Limitations and Reach Your Full Potential" in November 2014. As a Best-Seller Publisher, Anita helps people to put their positive perspectives into print.

PEACEFUL POINT by Darla Ouellette

#Peace is Found in the Heart

She walked into the house after a long and busy day. After quickly scanning the room and noticing that nothing had been done, she tried to take a deep breath. She had asked her son, what seemed like at least a dozen times, to pick up after himself, to clean his room, and do the chores he was expected to do. "Why does everything have to be so difficult?" she thought to herself as she put her coat away and tried to brace herself for any further messes that might be found. "He's been home alone all afternoon and evening... and I had left the list of chores to do. Why can't he just do as he's asked and get it done? And why can't he have a less moody and grumpy attitude and be more respectful?" She was at her wits end with him. She'd tried talking with him and letting him know that it isn't fair he treated her that way. It isn't right that he felt he could say and do what he wanted without thinking of her feelings.

Just as she walked into the living room, she noticed a single flower sitting on the coffee table, placed in a beautifully decorated vase. There was a note that read: *Dear mom, I didn't have time to do the chores you asked me to do. I did however notice this beautiful flower in your favorite color and it made me think of you. I promise I will do my chores tomorrow. I hope you like your flower. Love Cameron.*

She sat down on the couch, clutching the note. As tears streamed down her face, she gazed at the flower and felt peace in her soul once more. She had been so angry with him just moments ago. She had forgotten to remember what a gift he truly was. She had forgotten her peace. She had overlooked the harmony they had created together and that lives within their house.

She inhaled the lovely scent of the flower, feeling grateful once again and regained the peace within her heart. She loved her son more than anything and she knew he loved her too. There would surely be many more arguments and more stressful situations. But there would also be love and peace. She would make sure of it. Peace still dwelled within their home and in their hearts

Darla Ouellette is an accomplished Registered Nurse. She also holds diplomas for her RPN and Law and Security Administration. Darla is a devoted mother to her wonderful son Cameron, is certified as a Law Of Attraction Life Coach, and has always had a passion for writing.

https://ca.linkedin.com/pub/darla-ouellette

CHAPTER TWO by Chadi Hemaidan

Peace Will Give You Silence and Beauty Within

The first time I finally started to feel at peace was back in 2006. When I was introduced to one of my greatest mentors online, it was a period of my life when I was feeling discouraged and very close to depression. I was happily engaged, looking forward to starting a new life with someone I cared deeply about. Then, unexpectedly my fiancée and I broke up. Approximately a month later, after we went our separate ways, I opened my laptop looking for a song on the internet. Instead, I came across a life-changing video from a well-known mentor. At first I didn't know who exactly he was, so I listened to his message. He was a spiritual guru and his words of wisdom and motivation caused me to open myself up spiritually. I kept on listening to his messages and a few days later, I purchased my first motivational, inspirational book. This was the kind of encouragement and teachings that forever changed my life. Now, I always remember to carry positive affirmations with me throughout the day.

I became a spiritual person ten years ago. Prior to that, I lived a life of harsh negativity and was very judgmental of others. My old ego separated me from good things in life, like peace, positivity, gratitude, and even flowers. It also caused a lot of great people to walk out of my life. Ego even edged God out. I didn't know that at first, but now I do.

Most of the time, I was unhappy with myself, including the profession that I had. But now I have found a vocation that I love, and I appreciate what I am doing. When you are grateful and love what you are doing, you always feel blessed within your soul. You have to find value in what you are doing, and do what you find meaning and purpose in. This allows the source of divine peace to enter into your life.

When I started to practice mediation and yoga, I finally found peace, silence, and beauty within my soul. I find it gratifying to take walks every day. Each time, it's like a spiritual journey. I feel the love around me and the beauty of my inner-peace resonating with my surroundings. When I see nature in its fullness, I know that I am blessed because I can see, smell, feel, and touch the beauty of those butterflies floating and landing on those lovely flowers. Not everyone has this blessing, and for that, I am grateful to God for creating a beautiful world. I encourage you to walk with God daily, and you will feel the divine design of inner peace. This is the beauty of having some time for yourself to be within the creation of God.

I started to embrace my own inner peace, and found deep healing. Today, I choose to spread my positivity everywhere I go and with everyone I meet, accepting the things that now come my way. I walk with humility and because I've seen the light, I now allow it to shine brightly for others to be healed as well. The universe always opens a path for me to find strength for myself during times of difficulties. Since I've opened my heart to the universe, I cannot express in words the amount of healing and acceptance that has taken place. All I have to do to find the beauty of Mother Earth is to allow my pride to fall away.

My renewed faith in life inspired me to start doing new things, such as horseback riding for the last couple of years. My daily goal is to spend a quiet moment with nature, and to be in a state of now and appreciation. I sincerely believe that God created horses as divine creatures that speak to the human soul. I've also taken up hiking and these new passions have given me a new lease on life. I don't have time to waste feeling discouraged, sad, or negative any longer. My personal satisfaction comes from seeking out new adventures within my world around me. For instance, I've reach my highest view of the mountains that I have trekked, and enjoy seeing the view of the ocean, sitting in front of the lake, or simply watching the waterfalls. When you find yourself staring at the sunrise, or the sunset, you know that our Creator has got it all in control. There must be a higher purpose for this life, but first we have to find that inner peace, silence, and beauty from these divine creations of God.

My life's journey has taken me on a path of finding myself to discover things that were hidden deep within. As I've learned to embrace the things that come my way, I find exactly what I have been looking for. I've found my calling of helping others and am grateful for the skills I've learned, to listen to those around me. Whenever I meet strangers, I'm open to talking, listening, and encouraging them to connect within themselves so that they can also learn to appreciate their lives as well. My intentions are to continue working with the universe as a means to helping others. The road that I've traveled was not easy, but it led me to a path where I found my inner calling and life's purpose.

I believe I was given a miracle by finally seeing the meaning of life. As it turned out, my life's journey changed by finding one great teacher who helped me to understand that peace and healing comes from within. This abundance of peace and gratitude for life is located within our souls, and that is what removed my pride. My ego has now been humbled and is aware of how I want to live my life, by surrounding myself with spirit. I choose to attract more positive emotions into my life instead of isolating myself in the universe. I constantly work with happiness and compassion towards this life and the people I'm connected with in order to keep on giving the gift that God has given to me. It's amazing how we can all reach others from far away, and have these real connections to help others through various ways. You can reach your heart out towards the other side of the universe by helping one person with one touch of peace and beauty through the caring in your own words. I realize that I do not always know what is best for me, however I choose to believe the best will always come to me. We must always feel and live life from the heart. This is how I have chosen to learn about new ways from others.

I will open the gift of love that God has given me within my heart, and allow the creation of his love to embrace all that I do. As I permit myself to the universe, I'm learning the right way of walking my own path. This new awareness has given me the power to stay in control of my journey. I will keep on traveling, enjoying everything along the way. What I want to see must come from within me. I choose to spread my energy and light of positivity from the moment I wake up until I go to bed. I attract the things that I am and what will become of me. I embrace everything that comes to me.

Some of us have joyfully found peace in our lives, while sadly, so many others are still seeking it. Peace doesn't just happen in one's life by waiting around and expecting it to show up. For me, peace comes in many ways that I have already mentioned earlier. To find peace is finding yourself within our divine universe. I finally found my peace through practicing the art of silence and discovering the beauty in doing all those things. This special journey took me from who I was before, a self-centered, negative, and lonely man, and brought me to who I have become now, someone who values and appreciates everyone that I am blessed to be connected with. I use to block everything good that came my way. Now I understand why I must have peace within myself to attract the things I value and care for. This has greatly helped me to open myself to the unlimited universe.

Once I have peace, I will always attract beauty and happiness around me. There are many places you can go to find peace. However, I found my peace when I searched deep within my heart and soul. Peace is the instrument of love that brings me happiness. Peace to me is silence and beauty. Peace comes from God.

Chadi Hemaidan is a Personal Support Worker and a Teacher's Aide. He graduated from Canoga Park High School in 1991 where he was a member of the track and field team. Following high school, Chadi went to West Valley Occupational Center to study business. He has been caring for and assisting individuals with disabilities since he first volunteered at camp when he was eight years old, and has been working in the field of helping people for the past nineteen years. Chadi also volunteers working on one-to-one projects with adults and children, and enjoys composing poems and novels. He is pursuing his passion for writing.

Email: chemaidan@hotmail.com

Facebook: Chadi Hemaidan

PEACEFUL POINT by Tim Rahija

#Peace Through My Personal Perspective

Like many people, I used to believe (falsely) that the feeling of peace we experience in life is the result of some wonderful external experience, such as landing that great job, buying a new car, owning a home, etc. I would have to say, without a doubt, that which I have learned about life, happiness, peace, and what lies beyond stems from my own very near death experience of being shattered when struck by a car in 2010 and coming back from the brink of death with a much greater appreciation for life and all we have to be grateful for.

In my own studies and search for answers to help explain what I had been going through emotionally, mentally, and spiritually since that near death experience, I came to know some very awesome people that helped me gain a greater understanding of what was going on at the very fundamental, quantum level and it changed my life.

In this whole process which has been nothing more than a transition to a more enlightened and conscious self, I began to get a clear view of all that I had been raised to believe and value, and found most of it to be false because it was through the filters of others, although well intended. As a result of reading and research, and getting into ancient spiritual texts and traditions, did I begin to realize certain universal truths about what it is to experience peace in one's own life.

The most important thing I've learned and accepted as truth is that peace and happiness do not reside in the external world. The external world is just one more piece of the holographic universe we are all a part of. While we contribute to it, we are also a reflection of the greater whole. So, as we all change, the greater whole changes. So, if we want peace in the world and beyond, why do we not look to ourselves and create that template within, as it will be reflected in the whole since everything in space and time is connected at once?

I have personally validated time and again the miraculous power of the quantum universe in my own life that when I desire to experience peace in my life, I begin with the end in mind and set the mental picture of myself and the world at large at peace and I experience that reflection. It's really that simple but escapes most people because they are falsely conditioned into believing peace and happiness are only capable after achieving something in the external garbage they are inundated with on a daily basis.

Peace begins with you.

Tim Rahija is a Spiritual Entrepreneur and an International Best-Selling author. He has prior professional experience in Law Enforcement, US Army, Human Resource Management, Information Technology, and Aviation Maintenance. Tim is the founder of his own mobile application development company, with additional business ventures in other technology platforms, life coaching, and personal development.

timothy.rahija@gmail.com

CHAPTER THREE by Steve Yuzenko

The Missing "Peace"

What is peace? Is it an external environmental state? Is it an internal state? The answer to both questions is, yes! True peace is mostly an internal state, yet we cannot ignore the externalities that affect our peace. There are wars that can threaten our countries and even the world's security. There are states of non-peace that exist in our universe that we have yet to understand, even in the most obscure way. Since the universe includes ourselves, this is also true of us. We are as much a part of the universe as it is of us.

What do we all want? For the most part, we want to be happy, which includes a state of non-conflict, otherwise known as peace. So, to be happy, we need peace. Yet, even for some of the happiest people, there is something missing. They feel a general perception of well-being, and yet they believe it isn't a complete sense of happiness. What is it?

The "missing piece" is peace itself, hence called the "missing peace." Sometimes it's a general malaise, unidentifiable, an inner restlessness or even yearning that seems to elude identification. At other times, it has two horns, a pitched tongue and tail, and is glaring its red face brightly at us. In both instances, we seem to just sit there, in a state of non-acceptance, and also one of non-action. In this state, we will never achieve harmony, whether for ourselves, or for the universe.

What is a lack of peace? Is it war? Not necessarily! It could be as subtle as a queasy feeling in your gut when you think about something. The "lack of peace" is, in a way, a poverty of peace. We are in a state of peace-poverty when we are not experiencing peace fully. As true as it is individually, it is also true globally. Those of you, who experience financial poverty, if you've ever done so, know the multitude of feelings that contribute to your inner lack of serenity. You can't pay the mortgage, rent, car payments, credit card bill, or even worse, your medical or food bills. These unpeaceful feelings gnaw at our innards and even though we may have many other things in life, we feel this poverty deeply. We see this on a global scale as well. When nations have a great disparity of income, with a few being very wealthy and a majority of very financially poor citizens, there is a great lack of peace. The poverty factor is the piece that is missing in peace.

Other than financial poverty, there is emotional poverty, on a personal scale. You can have all of your financial needs met; and if your emotional needs are unmet, you are experiencing poverty, and again, a lack of peace. On a grander scale, if a population has their basic needs met, yet have unmet emotional needs (such as a lack of ability to care for the sick, malnourished, protect the insecure, or fear rather than trust in their workplace or government), they are in a state of poverty.

How do we find the missing peace? It may sound simple: just end poverty (on a personal or universal level) and we create peace. Okay, maybe not so "simple", eh? It can be though! So, where do we begin? We need to commence in the same place where any transformation starts, which is within our heart. You may be thinking, it's not me who needs to change; it is them who need to make the changes! To this, please don't be offended; I must say you are wrong. All change that we initiate must, to truly succeed, begin in our hearts. It must start in the depths of our souls, and be motivated from this place to affect the changes we need to make within and to ourselves before we can expand them to the world and the universe. Some people may think, "I can't change the world; I'll be lucky if I can make a change in myself." This statement has great truth, yet is a limited view. As we change ourselves, we can then let this transformation blossom and flourish. You may think, "How is a small change in me going to affect the world?" It's not easy. It will take more than "wishing" for world peace. It will take some work.

The work begins with a mindset shift, from poverty to wealth (not mere financial), and from a limited thought process to limitless one. Can you do this? If you answered yes, that's great! If you answered no, that's still great! Why? Well, if you can't make this change in yourself, there are others who can help you. The good part is, you don't necessarily need to pay for this outside help. Sure, if you have the resources for a professional coach or counselor, who will help you develop yourself from limited poverty to limitless wealth, by all means, utilize your resources to make that happen. Many people don't have those resources available to them. The good news is, that they don't need to let that factor stop them in their quest for liberation from whatever form of poverty that they are experiencing. There are others who can help. They are called friends!

How can friends help? They can assist you both with eliminating personal and universal poverty. Just as you have very powerful things within you, they are very powerful in their own unique ways! When you connect with someone, such as a friend, you each build a level of trust. There is a compassion and caring, which many times is unspoken yet known as clearly as if it were written across their foreheads. With a foundation of trust and compassion, you can break the barriers of inner limitation and remove poverty to gain untold riches in your life. We all have (or can have) friends like this!

Connection is the key! When you "connect" with a friend, a real friend (online or in person doesn't matter these days, as long as you both know the connection is genuine), they will naturally want to help you. What you don't realize is that your friend has resources within their capabilities (financial or otherwise) that you may not be aware of. They also have another valuable resource, which is a connection to other friends. You've heard the old saying "It's not what you know, it's who you know", right? These who's can be extremely powerful! Even more powerful than you have imagined.

So, how do I get started? The first thing to do may be the most difficult thing you've ever done. The first thing is to release your fear. Fear is almost the single most powerful emotion we have, second to love. It can paralyze us, and keep us from doing many things, including fulfilling our dreams. To release your fear, you need to recognize it, and then take action to release it. What action? Your action may be as simple as calling or reaching out to a friend, to have them begin the process of helping you to release the fear. Once you reach out, you have started a momentum that will immediately reduce the initial fear barrier. This is great! Oh, wait, but what if I don't have a friend to do this with? No problem! You need to reach out and connect with a (new) friend. Since we tend to attract and connect with those with whom we resonate with, start there. Introduce yourself (online or in person) to someone who you believe will eventually be a trusted friend. Sometimes this may take several introductions, yet you will find one, and then another, and another. I've seen this happen thousands of times! I've been part of an experiment to help connect people from, get this, foreign countries, on social media. Who in their right mind would connect to foreigners, many who don't even speak your language as their native tongue? Many people have done this and have created powerful global networks, which have not only eradicated personal poverty; it also helps many others to do the same. Doing this has even brought down borders between two countries, which powerful governments had erected, and great armies defended, yet both were powerless once individual connections between the two people in the two countries had been established.

Because of you, there will be no missing peace! You see, no border, no fear, no government, no corporation, no other person can combat the power within you, the power within your heart! Go out and connect and achieve limitless peace and love, my friends!

Yours in peace and love!

Steve Yuzenko is an author, speaker, and connection expert. Married for over thirty years, he and his wife have three wonderful kids. Steve is an International Best-Selling author, who coaches and consults in areas of personal development, health & fitness, information technology, and businesses growth & improvement, from single-person startups to multi-million and multi-billion dollar corporations. With degrees in Marketing, Business Administration, Accounting, and Computer Science, combined with over twenty years of executive level experience in industries ranging from manufacturing to logistics & cold chain optimization, he offers a breadth of skills and value for a wide variety of industries.

Website: www.wholepreneur.com

Facebook: Facebook/Wholepreneur

PEACEFUL POINT by Marigrace Galura

#Peace is How You Make It

Where does peace begin? From my experience, it always comes from within. We are easily influenced with various messages and images brought to us by the media. It's up to us to discern what we choose to fill our minds with. Whether we like it or not, we can be easily bogged down with negative messages that will ultimately affect us. I like to make time for myself to reflect or check on what's happening around me. Is there peace existing in my current environment? If not, I try to visualize something that brings back peaceful memories: trees, green grass, flowers, grey clouds, rain, sunshine, and being near the lake. Then I immerse myself into it visually by adding my other senses, such as what I can feel, touch, and taste, making me feel relaxed and at peace. The perfect example was when I had taken a mini vacation in my own city of Toronto, Canada. I didn't have to go very far, but I made my visualization come to life and live it. The results were incredible. I felt calm, relaxed, and achieved my inner peace.

The feeling of calmness gives you the clarity your mind deserves. You can accomplish anything. What is your vision of Peace? You can start by using pictures you have from print or online to make your vision board of Peace. When creating my own, I found a picture of the peace sign carved in sand from a beach. I then posted it on all of my social media accounts with #PEACE. Magic happens when you know your vision and take action towards it. A year later, I was more accepting of myself and forgave my past. I now treat myself with the same kindness that I give to others. Today, a more peaceful Marigrace has emerged and the opportunity to contribute to this special anthology came into fruition.

Thoughts really become things. They are powerful. Choose to think with Peace. It will create miracles you have never imagined. My hope is to let you know that Peace from within sets you free from your own barriers that you carry inside. When you are feeling light and happy, you can create your own peaceful world. Everyone around you will thank you for it. Peace is within you!

Marigrace is a Fashion Accessories Artist and designer who handcrafts jewelry with insight to peoples' personalities. Her goals are to have others express themselves creatively and ignite their unique personal style. Marigrace enjoys empowering others through storytelling and sharing experiences.

Social Media: https://www.facebook.com/MarigraceAccessoriesInc

CHAPTER FOUR by Elani Kay

Peace and Tranquility is Still Possible

Picture a beautiful, crisp, blue and turquoise flowing river of water slowly moving by in front of you. As you gaze at the moving water, imagine you feel a nice gentle breeze brushing itself ever so softly along your face, leaving you with a sense of peace and comfort. The sun is shining warmly upon your body, surrounding you with a feeling of safety and strength. Around you are colors of nature's beauty, from the bright purple lilacs to the gorgeous greens of the trees and grass. You feel open, comfortable, happy, and free. As you slowly inhale, your only concern at that moment is to embrace the feeling of life entering your body. This is peace. Peace is a feeling.

Life is the result of the choices we make, and when we are at an internal peaceful place, our choices reflect that. The truth is that our outer world is a reflection of our inner world. I personally never understood this until I realized that I had allowed my outer world to completely control and affect my inner world. I didn't know at the time that it was supposed to be the other way around. You see, peace is possible when you are no longer fighting a battle within yourself. Every person is engaged in some internal battle and when that war is over, peace is felt.

It can be a struggle trying to figure out our individuality and who are we in this world. Growing up, I was constantly questioning myself and as a result I was doing things I knew I really didn't want to do. Living life like that made me a very confused and frustrated person. I would attract other people who were like me and together we would create more confusion. I also would pay more attention to things that further confused and frustrated me. Most of my life was spent focusing on problems versus solutions, drama versus progress, and setbacks versus breakthroughs. What I focused on became my reality. Peace was not even a thought, nor did I think about wanting peace.

Have you ever had to make a discussion with yourself where you can't decide whether or not you want to be the bigger person in a situation or confront the situation head on regardless of the consequences? That was how I was.

That is an example of the internal battle that people deal with because they are not sure who they are yet and as a result they allow people and events to influence the choices they make.

For me, when the noise of life got so loud to the point that I no longer felt free was when I knew it was time for a change. I wanted to be able to experience the unexpected and not allow it to affect or influence my emotions in a negative way. I wanted to learn how to remain joyful when someone else was intentionally trying to bring me down. I wanted to feel a sense of calmness when everything around me was chaotic. I wanted peace.

Peace is possible when the sounds of the world no longer drown out the sounds of your soul. When I decided I was ready to live my life by what was in my heart and my soul first, I simply no longer concerned myself with things I had no control over. I stopped listening to voices of doubt, negativity, and the chaos that had taken over my life. Each day I would find more things to celebrate and to appreciate. Through my experiences, I learned that the more peace I found within myself, I became a person that could live at peace with others regardless of how they treated me. I made a definitive decision that I would no longer allow the behavior of others to destroy and affect my inner peace.

Days, months, and years would go by and as more things happened to test me, I only got better at it. Like many things in life, the more we do it, the better we get. I am by no means perfect, but I can smile now through pain and the rain. Situations like angry or dangerous drivers on the road no longer affect me, negative put downs no longer phase me, or even people with extreme anger who may threaten me no longer evoke a negative reaction from me. I do understand how challenging it is to be at peace with yourself, so I can only empathize with all the people out there struggling with this. Peace does not mean that we are at a place where there is no noise or problems; peace means to be surrounded by many things and still be able to be at peace in your heart. Accepting things as they are through the act of understanding makes peace possible, and I am so thankful for that.

Elani Kay is the mother of three young boys, an entrepreneur, a mommager, a Talent Life Coach, author, and the Operations Coordinator for an Entertainment Company and a Business Consulting Firm in the USA. Originally from a background of providing Applied Behavior Analysis Therapy for autistic children, Elani has brought with her the skills she acquired as an ABA Therapist to help the many young adults she works with today as a mentor and life coach. She also has served on the board for a non-profit organization that serves youth for the past five years, including successfully raising capital to help save domestically trafficked youth.

Website: www.elanikay.com

CHAPTER FIVE by Elizabeth Ann Pennington

Peaceful Perceptions from Pain Are Still Possible

Peace is a word used by multitudes. It's used or thought of in our day-to-day lives. I know I've said many a time, "I would love to have just a little peace and quiet." How many of you have said the same? It's only my opinion but I would say everyone reading this has at one time or other wished for peace in some respect of their lives.

The meaning of peace can differ from person to person; it depends on the need or circumstances around each individual. What does peace look like to you? It could be a reprieve from war. Maybe you need a more tranquil place to live, away from an aggressive neighborhood. Perhaps you're asking for a peaceful settlement in a messy divorce. In my case, I needed peace of mind, body, and soul from a lifetime of events stacked one on top of another.

I thought, like a lot of other people I know, that peace was some-thing you have when you settle an argument or come home from a long day at work and enjoy resting quietly in your recliner. Once you have reached success, you possess everything you need to start enjoying the serene life you have dreamed of. Peace sometimes is thought of as a destination. I believe our culture has a big influence on our view of peace. Society has made it external in-stead of internal.

I've had many heartbreaking circumstances and events in my life, but they were just part of life's stepping stones to becoming a stronger person.

We all think life is over when we lose the first love of our lives. Then we discover life goes on. We lose a job or jobs, causing financial burdens, but somehow we make it. We watch television and see all the terrible things going on around the world and wonder why can't something be done to stop it.

Throughout our lives, we face one event after the other that disturbs the peace we have in life. It's how we handle these events that will make the difference between having peace or not.

Sometimes a child may have traumatic events happen to them that a parent or caretaker does not either recognize or may not know how to help the child. This happened to me when I was seven years old and my father passed away. He was more than my father; he was my best friend. When he passed away, I blamed myself. If it was a school day, I always gave him a hug and kiss before I went in the house to change out of my school clothes into play clothes. If it was not a school day and he was at work, I still went to see him approximately the same time each day. I don't have a memory of him not being at work.

On the day of his passing, a playmate was going to be staying at our house for the night. I was so excited, and before I raced into the house, I told my bother to say "Hi" to Daddy for me. As my grandmother was helping me with the zipper in the back of my dress, my brother came racing into the house screaming frantically of our father's demise.

As far as I was concern, I had caused my Daddy to pass away from a broken heart. I didn't take time to give him a hug and kiss when I came home from school that day. When I was a little older, I was told Daddy had died from a heart attack, but it didn't help much. What still remained in my mind was that I had broken his heart. It was not until much later in life when I made the statement of how I felt in front of my brother that he replied, "You didn't, I did." After a long discussion with my brother, knowing that he had also felt responsible for our father's fate, I begin to heal.

In my teen years I was sexually abused. I held it as a secret until a few years ago. The reasoning I gave myself to keep it hidden was shame. As I became an adult, I wanted to talk about what had happen to me but couldn't think of anyone I could trust to keep my secret private, not even a professional. I lived in a small community and people talked. So, I convinced myself it would be wrong to tell. All I could think about was the shame and hurt it would bring to my family. You see, the perpetrator had convinced me that if I told anyone, I would be accused of causing it to happen, and I would be looked at as a very bad and shameful girl. I justified not talking by asking myself that if I was to talk to someone, would it change anything? Was it going to make it all better or give me back the years I had loss being afraid of receiving affection?

The feeling of betrayal and hurt I lived with all those years caused bitterness. I found it hard to get close to people, especially males; I had loss trust, even in myself. I had no peace as this offence found a way to affect everything in my life.

Five years into our marriage, my husband and I decided to start a family. After a couple years we were sitting in the waiting room of an infertility doctor. A few more years passed by. We were referred to a group of specialist that worked with couples needing more than the traditional procedures. We tried everything possible to get pregnant including drugs that were in the testing phrases. I experienced side effects, vision problems, from one of the drugs and was rushed to doctor for treatment. The drugs were stopped and my sight came back. It was very frightening when I suddenly could only see straight out in front of me but I will never regret trying.

My husband and I went through the whole array of procedures including surgery without anyone knowing. No one could know we were trying artificial insemination. The final straw came when I experienced false pregnancy. Into what would have been the third month I was awakened with pain and was lying in a pool of blood. The stress of it all was too much and was time to stop.

You may be asking yourself what does our not having children have to do with peace. If you are someone who has children, it will be a little harder to understand how devastating it is to be told that you won't be able to conceive a child. If you have been told you will not conceive, then you will be more understanding. One of the things that I dislike, coming from people with children, is "You're lucky you don't have children." Please...walk in my shoes before you say that to anyone.

You may be wondering why we didn't adopt. We didn't because we had a conflict with family acceptance of children that would have not been our maternal children. We simply could not bring a child into a situation where they would have not been welcomed equally to the other children in the family.

Later in life we realized we should have resolved the conflict instead of trying to please others. We unfortunately let others make a choice about our life, that should have been only ours to make. The action we took kept us from the pleasure, enjoyment, and love of our own family. It took a long time and effort to move forward and find peace from that decision. If only we could all see into the future.

I recall another disturbing event when I had car engine failure while traveling on the interstate. I was between exits and by myself. I raised the hood of the car as I had been told to do so someone knows you have car trouble. I got back in the car and waited. I didn't have a cell phone at that time. I saw officials pass by and of course hundreds of other cars. No one was stopping to see if I needed help. I had made sure all windows were up. I let the driver's side window down only enough for fresh air and to talk if anyone stopped. While I waited I found a piece of paper and pen in the glove department and made a list of phone numbers I could give to whoever stopped.

Finally, there was a car pulling in behind me. When the man approached my car and asked if he could help, I ask if he had a phone or if he could go to a phone and call the numbers I had listed. He said he would, took my list, and left. Two hours later no one came. It was getting dark so I begin to worry.

While looking for the paper and pen I had come across a knife. I pulled it out and laid it in on the console for anyone to see and I waited. I had been writing down the time as it passed and things that I had saw. I had written about the man that had stopped and how no help had returned. While I waited, I wrote a note to say goodbye to my love ones in case I didn't make it.

Someone else finally stopped and it looks as if the vehicle was an official of some kind. The man approached my side of the car and asked me to let the window down, but I refused. He tried to convince me he couldn't talk to me if I didn't let the window down, but I continued to refuse. He told me what kind of official he was and that I was safe. I asked him through the opening if he would call someone that would be able to come get me. He said he had a radio and would call anyone I wanted called.

As he went back to his vehicle, I relaxed. After a few minutes I looked in the rear view mirror to see what was taking him so long, but I couldn't see him. I looked in the door mirrors on both sides – no one. I turned as much as possible but could not see him anywhere. Then all of a sudden he appeared on the passenger side of the car. I tried staying as clam as I could, but was thinking the worse.

After a moment or two, even though it seems like hours, he returned to his vehicle and left. I had grabbed my pen and paper to write down the license plate number as he pulled away so I could report him, but to my surprise the license plate was missing. I knew then why I had not been able to see him. He had been removing the license plate so I couldn't make note of it.

Hours passed before I was rescued. By this time, I was in shock so when I was touched, my body began to shake as I burst in tears and couldn't stop crying for a very long time. I felt dirty and frightened. I felt like I had been violated. Several people asked what had happened. When I told them, I was laughed at. This was another event in my life I pushed deep inside. It took time but I forgave those people and came to grips with the whole situation in order to receive peace from the mental anguish.

One late sleepless night I made a decision to not only tell someone but to tell the world. I had been invited to contribute to an anthology project that was being complied. The subject I was to write about was healing, a true story about something that had happened in my life, how it had affected my life, and how I had dealt with it. That struck a chord. I wrote about the molestation, how I had forgiven the person and then forgave myself, and how this was healing to my mind, body and soul. I was crying the whole time I was composing that account. Writing about it was healing but what I didn't know was that I needed more. I needed peace of mind.

When I saw my story in print, it became reality. I felt relief. I realized I had released this tragic event; it was no longer a secret and was going to be read around the globe. I was able to let it go. I felt the shame leave my body that day, giving me hope and peace of mind that my story might help someone else release the fear, embarrassment, bitterness, or low self-esteem they might be holding onto.

As I have mentioned, peace is not something you reach out and touch. You don't find it in the material things of life. Peace is a state of mind and comes from within. Peace is within our power and is our choice. Reach in and pull the hidden burdens from deep within yourself. Don't be afraid of asking for help. I still deal with some issues today but with help from doctors and God on my side, I am able to keep an open mind that one day I will find peace from them as well. Each day, week, and year gets a little easier to handle.

I have been amazed at the things I had hidden away, afraid of facing them. Not knowing how to deal with them, I stacked them on top of each other to silence them in my mind. The problem is the subconscious is always at work whether you're aware of it or not. I had been afraid of asking for help but once I admitted I needed it, I didn't turn back and am I so grateful now.

A while ago, I had a long trip to make. I had a session with my doctor a few days before and made a lot of progress that day. It had opened more questions which was a good thing. As I traveled I had time to think. I was looking at God's creations of both beauty and flaws of the land. A flood of clarity washed over me like a tidal wave. We are each a creation of God and no different from the land I was admiring. We have beauty and we have flaws. My aha moment! All I had to do was stop holding onto things out of my control – declutter the cluttered.

From my own experience, looking for peace through my depressions, anxieties, disappointments, heartaches, feelings of worthlessness, fears, and lack of energy, there is one thing I will ask of you: Don't give up! There is indeed a light at the end of your tunnel.

Elizabeth Ann Pennington is a Certified Life Coach, Best-Selling International Author, Speaker, Trainer and Mentor. Elizabeth is also a co-author in *"Living Without Limitations – 30 Mentors to Rock Your World!"*, *"Living Without Limitations- 30 Stories to Heal Your World"*, *"#Love – A New Generation of Hope"*, *"#Love – A New Generation of Hope Continues..."* and *"Living Without Limitations – Vision Quest."* She received her coaching certificate from School of Coaching Cognition, is a member of ICF, and trained as an internet marketer with School of Online Business. Elizabeth agrees that traditional education is very important, but sees life's experience as irreplaceable.

Email; eapennington@outlook.com

FaceBook: http://www.facebook.com/elizabeth.a.pennington

PEACEFUL POINT by Malini Siva

#Peace is the Love of My Child

The word "Peace" takes a different form based on the perspective of each individual. For some, it's the silence that comes after chaos while for others, it's the feeling of accomplishment. It may mean job satisfaction, a casual conversation with a friend, or even spending time with a loved one.

The most accomplished and happiest moment of my life was realized after the discovery of my pregnancy with my first and only son. It created a wonderful and everlasting joy and peace that surpassed all my other happiness and accomplishments including graduating from university, getting my first job, buying my first car, or even buying my first home. It was something extraordinary and quite a magical moment where I felt like I'd conquered the world. As I closed my eyes, I saw so much peace, happiness, and unconditional love.

My son inspired me to touch the heights I never thought were even possible in my life. I established myself in my career, became PMP certified, and was able to manage complex projects. I was able to handle stress, solve issues, and think strategically to come up with solutions. I was loved by everyone around me. I found the peace within my self-extending its full arms to people who were in need and offered a hand in every way possible to help. It helped me to open my mind and heart to people and also healed the wounds within my heart.

With a million things going wrong, one thing that keeps me happy and puts a smile on my face is the moment I see my son running into my arms, hugging me so tight, and kissing me. I only ever need his laughter to refresh my brain and to feel the clarity in my mind. All the pain, struggles, and worries are released and I return to a neutral state. I am reminded that I have a purpose and to keep moving forward, irregardless.

We are all unique individuals. Therefore, we need to find what brings our souls to peace, make sure we give space for ourselves to grow, and touch many more souls in this life. I came to the realization that without accepting the present moment as is and being grateful for all the things life has to offer, one can never be peaceful in life. I take full responsibility for all the decisions that I have made in life, and also accept the consequences. This made such a huge difference in the way I see life. I take nothing for granted.

With that being said, my life is very beautiful and so colorful! I can assure you, that yours will be too!

We are all unique individuals. Therefore, we need to find what brings our souls to peace, make sure we give space for ourselves to grow, and touch many more souls in this life. I came to the realization that without accepting the present moment as is and being grateful for all the things life has to offer, one can never be peaceful in life. I take full responsibility for all the decisions that I have made in life, and also accept the consequences. This made such a huge difference in the way I see life. I take nothing for granted. With that being said, my life is very beautiful and so colorful! I can assure you, that yours will be too!

Malini Siva is a Project Manager, Quality Assurance Analyst and a mother of a four-year-old handsome boy. She graduated from Ryerson University in 2005 with a B.Sc in Computer science. Afterwards, she pursued the Project Management Professional (PMP) credentials from PMI in 2015.

CHAPTER SIX by Pamela Kunopaskie

Five Habit to Finding Inner Peace

Traditionally, inner peace, or peace of mind, has been defined (by means of various resources) as a state of being mentally and spiritually at peace, armed with enough knowledge and understanding to keep oneself strong when times get tough.

When we think of people who have truly mastered the art of inner peace, names like Buddha, Mother Theresa, and Gandhi are ever present. This chapter is dedicated to everyone else.

The following five habits can be used by anyone to master inner peace. These routines are meant to act as a guide to those who realistically don't have the time to diligently reflect and meditate for more than one hour a day and when faced with a major adversity, will have an emotional breakdown. It is also for those who would just love to see an extra hour added to each day so that they can complete that last task before the new day begins.

In order to achieve personal harmony, we have must be armed with enough knowledge and understanding when times get tough. How does one acquire these two attributes? Knowledge and understanding are generated from two sources; from within and from external experiences. Inner peace is more than sitting in silence, meditating. It comes from getting out in the world and experiencing life! Many people fail to realize that this is a personal choice. We choose the level of peace that we allow ourselves to experience.

To me, inner peace is the discovery of a waterfall that I never knew existed, or a conversation with the person sitting next to me on a subway just to see if maybe we have something in common. Harmonious equilibrium is obtained by doing rather than being. In other words, you can't just say that you're going to obtain inner peace and "voila," you have it. It's acquired by making changes, experiencing new perspectives, feeling a myriad of emotions, and at the end of it all, realizing that regardless of what happens in life, you are life.

Habit #1 - Stop watching the clock and make time for things that make you happy.

As we get older, many of us worry if we're going to have enough time in a day to get things done, time in our lives to accomplish our set goals, time enough to do this and to do that. Stop it! Time can only be appreciated by each second that we live it. We need to understand that nothing is more important than what we do with the time we are given right now. Yes, it is amazing to have goals and strive to achieve them; but also understand that Rome was not built in a day! Allow yourself the time to accomplish goals and stop beating yourself up if they take a little longer.

Go for a walk, have a night out with your friends, or sit alone on the beach and read a book. It is in these moments that we allow peace to enter our lives naturally and rejuvenate our souls so that we can continue to live life authentically.

To sum it up: Do things that make you content. Experiencing happy moments that make you grow emotionally, mentally, and spiritually will give you a broader reality of life and create a platform where peace can manifest with the littlest of effort needed.

Habit #2 – Be open to new experiences.

How many people have a bucket list? The majority of these lists of life-time goals include some pretty amazing adventures ranging from hiking the sand dunes in the Sahara Desert, to diving the Great Blue Hole in Belize. Bucket lists are a great way keep track of what we want to accomplish in our lives, however, one fundamental component fails to appear on most bucket lists: attainable experiences for short-term daily or weekly time periods. If you walk to work, take a different route once a week. If you are out shopping, compliment someone who is trying on a new jacket. If you are in an elevator start up a conversation with a complete stranger about how their day is going.

New experiences expand your boundaries. According to the latest research done by Peter Caprariello and Harry Reis in 2013, their study was published in the Journal of Personality and Social Psychology Research and showed that experiences make us happier because we get to share our memories with others. New people and new surroundings enable us to grow and acquire knowledge from sources that would not have otherwise been part of our lives. To further elaborate on the importance of having experiences, a collection of studies further revealed that even unpleasant experiences, such as getting lost in a wood, or a rainy camping holiday, are later valued more than material possessions.

To sum it up: New experiences present opportunities for grow and align you with your destiny. Once you observe this ideal equilibrium around yourself, you will realize that the world is perfectly balanced, both within and without. Only then are you able to forge your own destiny and allow the enlightened part of you to direct your life, rather than let yourself be run by your fears.

Habit #3 – Experience your mistakes whole-heartedly.

"The only mistake in life is the lessons not learned." This quote by Einstein is one of my favorite quotes of all time. We are humans and were born to make mistakes. Usually the mistakes we make give rise to deep-seeded lessons and truths that propel personal growth.

By understanding that a mistake or a failure is human nature, that it is part of life, we stop striving for perfection and start accepting that we are perfection in the making. If we are always trying to live a "mistake-free" life, we will rarely acquire inner peace because we will never be good enough in our own eyes.

The next time you make a blunder, look at it with wonder and crave to know what lesson you are learning at that moment. When we look at mistakes in such a light, they do not become personal or reflect who we are, but rather they reflect the person who we are about to become.

To Sum it up: Mistakes can fuel our awareness. In helping us decide how to act and react in a fresh and fruitful way, they can bring us closer to happiness and further away from (causing our own) suffering. Less suffering leaves room for increased inner peace.

Habit #4 - Know that everything is connected and there is a greater plan.

Everything happens for a reason. Some call it destiny, some call it karma, others may call it synchronicity, but at the end of the day, everything that you have experienced in your life, the good, the bad, the crazy exciting stuff, the calm mellow moments, all have happened not by chance but rather by reason. Each situation that presents itself into your life is the foundation of what is yet to come. Without that one event, the next event could not occur.

Knowing that every experience in your life has been carefully orchestrated to fulfill your divine purpose, inner peace is created by knowing all things are as they should be. Once you realize that you do not need to be in control of your situations, you will be set free. You now accept that everything is part of a larger plan and things will happen with or without your consent.

> *To sum it up: By knowing that everything is connected and will happen in perfect timing, we give up the feeling of desperation and living a life in fear. Inner peace is created knowing that all things will work out as they should according to our divine purpose.*

Habit #5 – Create goals with deadlines.

Life is busy. From the moment we wake up until we go to bed, there are always things to do or places to be. In order to make the most of our time, goals are needed to keep us on track. Having goals are a necessity in finding inner peace for five reasons.

First off, goals give you focus. You can have all the potential in the world but without focus your abilities and talent are useless.

Secondly, goals allow you to measure progress. By setting goals you are able to measure your progress because you always have a fixed endpoint or benchmark to compare with. Achievement creates peace of mind.

Third, goals keep you locked in and undistracted. Goals give you mental boundaries. When you have a certain end point in mind, you automatically stay away from certain distractions and stay focused towards the goal.

Fourth, goals help you overcome procrastination. When you set a goal for yourself, you make yourself accountable to finish the task.

And finally, goals give you motivation. The root of all the motivation or inspiration you have ever felt in your entire life was fueled by goals. Goal setting provides you the foundation for your drive. It gives you something to focus on and put 100% of your effort into. This focus is what develops motivation.

> *To sum it up: Peace of mind comes from knowing that we are contributing to our own well-being and the well-being of others in a timely, structured manner that our brains can process with ease.*

Life is full of surprises. We control how we respond to them, and the best way to strike a balance is to roll with the punches and go with the flow. Life's unpredictable course is our opportunity to meet surprises with acceptance and grace. Inner peace is a choice that we all have. By choosing to explore and experience life with no expectations, we are able to find that perfect balance between what is and what will be.

Pamela Kunopaskie is a Connections Anthropologist, Medium, and Intuitive. She has served as a senior consultant to leading 9-1-1 telecommunications and air traffic control providers, as well as owned and operated three retail chain stores. She has worked with both Provincial and Federal Governments helping small businesses succeed. Pamela taught Marketing, Law, Business Communications, and Human Resources at college level. She has worked for two of Canada's largest retail enterprises, helped guide and connect hundreds of individuals to their authentic self, and traveled extensively throughout North America. Pamela has a plethora of knowledge for business and life.

PEACEFUL POINT by Sabinah Adewole

#Peace is Pampering Yourself

I am at peace the most when I go on vacation with my family and we either tour the country side or do other relaxing things like a boat trip or a mini cruise.

I am at peace the best when I am outdoors. I enjoy walking, cycling, the green scenery, and driving along country lanes. I especially appreciate the sky, the sun, and the wind. I take in every little detail around me.

I am at peace when it is quiet and I can hear a pin drop or the clock tick.

I am at peace when I read a book I enjoy. I recently read a book on Mindfulness and I've learnt how to manage my panic attacks successfully.

I am at peace when I have a relaxed conversation with someone I connect with and we are on the same wavelength.

I am at peace when I attend my Yoga and Pilates classes and I am able to take a deep breath without having to think about why I am doing it or what I am doing at that moment.

I am at peace as I went and studied beauty therapy which covered areas of skin types and massage techniques.

I am at peace when I have a massage on holidays. I enjoy massages and have had massages across many countries that I have visited.

I am at peace at my best when I am in the sauna, steam bath, and Jacuzzi.

I am at peace as I set up my own Spa business abroad and we had executives from banks and other hotels come in for massages, facials, and other types of treatments.

I was involved in a Healthy-Life business which was directed at well-being and healthy lifestyle which, again without peace, you cannot achieve these goals.

I am at peace when I enjoy all the above, I feel that I have a balanced lifestyle, and I can take on any challenges or opportunities of self-discovery that arise.

I am at Peace when I am in church and have the opportunity to praise the Lord. I let go and believe I am with God. I am relaxed in mind, body, and spirit. I am relaxed because the presence of God is with me.

Mastering the art of breathing

It is found in the ordinary, the obvious, the mundane, and the exotic. All it means is bringing your attention and awareness to everything and everyone around you. Even as your mind starts wandering off to its next command, you can bring it back to the now by taking a breath and paying attention to it – unhurriedly – just as it is.

And take another breath just for good measure.

Sabinah Adewole is an International Best-Selling Author who studied English Literature. She was a co-author in the anthology "The Depth of her Soul – Beautiful Stories of Faith and Empowerment" which became a Best-Seller on Amazon.com. Her first book "All that Glitters" is being published, and she has started writing her second book entitled "The Fall of the Legend."

CHAPTER SEVEN by Stephanie Roy

Recognizing Peace in the Lowest of Places

There are many ways peace can be achieved. Some obtain it through meditation, yoga, or even just being out in nature. My personal feeling of peace began with a dream. I guess what makes my experience different is that mine was not sought after, but thrown at me like a snowball to the face. This may sound like a bad experience, but it was in fact the most positive and beautiful episode of my life because it gave me the wakeup call I needed to change my life.

I was a born introvert, coupled with an antisocial, awkward, and often sullen behavior. I was the kid you either didn't notice or just tried to avoid. I was an even more unhappy teenager as I also became solitary and self-conscious, like most teenage girls I guess.

Although I was an exceptionally bright high school student, I dropped out early just because I couldn't handle being around other students. I was able to falsely justify my bad decision with the fact that I met and moved in with the first man who asked me. He was ten years older than me and had a three-year-old child, so I thought my life plan would be to get married, live the white picket lifestyle, have a bunch of kids, and never have to worry about being around people, ever. I'm not saying I thought being a stay-at-home mom would be easy; quite the opposite. I just knew it would be easier to be around people I knew and not have to worry about dealing with strangers or anything different. It was my escape from life. I also always cherished the idea of loving and being loved unconditionally by children. And I loved my step-son like my own, so I knew I would always keep that motherly instinct.

When I had my first miscarriage during our first year of living together, I was twenty years old. It nearly destroyed me. I eventually had a total of six miscarriages in a row, all occurring at nine and a half weeks each time. By now, I was angrier than ever before. I couldn't understand how crackheads were pumping out babies without even trying, and here was I, who took every precaution—didn't drink or smoke, and I couldn't fulfill the basic requirement of what made being a woman special. This was how I felt at the time.

The night before my last miscarriage, I had a dream that would plant the seed of inner peace, and would change my life forever. I went to bed that night the same way I always did, hopeful for the future. This pregnancy seemed different to me since I was a little further along than before: I was at ten weeks. In the dream, all I could see was white. I suddenly heard a voice, but not really. The best way to explain is that I couldn't hear with my ears as much as feel with all my senses. It was female, and very soothingly she expressed to me, "I am so sorry Stephanie, but you will lose this baby also." At this point I could hear something – it was me crying. Then she said to me, "But don't be sad because you are not meant to have children. You are meant to do something later that does not require any distraction." I awoke soon after to a feeling of calmness I had not experienced before. I was very quiet that day, contemplating, afraid of what would happen next, but was prepared for once. I had the miscarriage later that day as expected. I was uncharacteristically calm, and I could not get that dream out of my mind. I started to question where my life would lead. I was starting to think that maybe I wasn't meant to have children; that it wasn't my intended life's direction.

Life went on, and a few months later, another unexpected event happened. Afterwards, I decided that finishing high school was the first step in accomplishing that goal, and I was happy for the first time in a long time, feeling as if I was really doing something. As I was having a shower to get ready for class, I felt a sudden stabbing pain in my chest, the worst physical pain ever. As I doubled over in the spray of the water thinking I was about to die, I started to panic but then something told me that it was important to stay calm. After I realized whatever it was it couldn't be a heart attack since I was a healthy twenty-three year old who didn't drink or do drugs, I did just that. The feeling subsided to a dull pain, so I went to school. After much coaxing from my sister, I went to the hospital. Because I was so calm, I was at first misdiagnosed as having a stress episode and sent home. After a week of seeing the doctor, it was discovered with much dismay that I was actually having an aortic aneurysm! The only reason I was still alive was because I had calmed myself down initially, which actually caused the blood to clot around the hole in my aorta. The doctors were shocked at this, but my family was probably more shocked at my behavior afterwards.

I was twenty-three when I died. I realize that may sound a bit over-dramatic, but that's what happened. The old me died and the new me emerged like a butterfly from a constricted cocoon. It was if some Higher Power hit a restart button and gave me a second chance. After a risky open heart surgery, where the doctor explained before I was anesthetized that I had a ten percent chance of survival – which was being generous, I awoke to the most euphoric feeling of joy I can hardly explain. It was then that the doctor explained there was good news and bad news. The good news was that I was alive; the bad news was that I would never be able to have children.

He explained that although there was still no explanation for my past miscarriages, they were actually a blessing in disguise. I was diagnosed with a genetic heart defect which meant my connective tissue was the same consistency as overcooked spaghetti, and if I had gone further than four months into a pregnancy, it would have killed both me and the baby.

I believe this was the moment when my personality snapped. Maybe it was the joy of being impossibly alive, mixed with the sadness of never being able to know the feeling of pregnancy, but sometimes I think it also removed the burden and pressure of having children. I felt a hidden, almost guilty relief. I was so happy I couldn't sleep, and refused any and all medication including pain meds for fear of subduing this joyous feeling. I stayed awake and cried for three days, talking continuously which was out of character for me since I was usually so shy and withdrawn. My husband was there for me physically, but not emotionally. Every time I tried to explain how I felt, he would tell me to be quiet because I sounded like a crazy person. I realized then that I didn't love him, and possibly never did. I understood that I loved the idea of having a family of my own, but not with him. He was cruel and treated me like a child. In retrospect, I suppose I was in a way, but I was raising his child and he never once acknowledged this fact. He just expected me to do my duties quietly. I comprehended that for my life to be complete, he could never be a part of it.

It was in the hospital where I first felt what real peace was. But I realized that for me to continue feeling it, I had some major changes to make. Getting an education was a beginning, but I had to leave my husband. Unfortunately, leaving my stepson was going to make this difficult since I loved him like my own. I made the naive mistake of thinking my husband would let me leave quietly and allow me custody rights. How wrong I was. If there is one sad aspect to this story, it's that my stepson was taken away from me so that I have not been able to see him for over ten years, all because of petty spite. There are still times when I wonder if I should have stayed at least for him, but that would have been worse. A child knows when a parent is unhappy and with him seeing his father treat me badly, I did not want him to grow up thinking that was the way a man should treat a woman. We speak now (my stepson and I) but it's not the same. Too much damage has been done.

Afterwards, I lived a life of ultimate freedom; ups and downs, accomplishments and failures. I even spent some time in jail which was, unbelievably, a wonderful learning experience which I will never regret. I even helped some women along the way which was exactly what I felt I was meant to do all along. I myself learned that peace can only be achieved with the understanding that there are sacrifices to be made along the way. In the words of a famous musician, "You can't always get what you want, but if you try sometimes, you might just find, you get what you need." When you think about it in the bigger picture, we have peace in our country achieved how? With war many years ago. How's that for irony? We have free speech which is an amazing thing even though that means having to tolerate speech we don't always want to hear. Freedom and peace is a double-edged sword. I guess what that dream was trying to tell me all those years ago was that to achieve ultimate peace and enlightenment, you have to accept that there will be a price to pay. Once you have accepted and understand this, only then can you relax and enjoy your life fully and wholeheartedly.

So, how can you achieve this feeling of ultimate peace? Stop depriving yourself and take some chances even if it means you may have to pay for it. Just make sure it's worth it. And always enjoy the little things. So, jump fully clothed into that pool, eat that butter smothered lobster, drink that wine, talk to that stranger. And remember, there are worse things than death. It's called life without living.

Stephanie Roy is an aspiring author who graduated from Algoma University in 2011 with a BA in Psychology and a Minor in English Literature. Her goal is to understand human nature and has been trying to accomplish this endeavor by being employed in as many different occupations as possible including taxi driver, carnival worker, actress, and youth worker in high risk areas. Stephanie currently resides in Montreal, Quebec with her dog Sadie, and is working on an autobiography about her sister who passed away from cancer, and the impact this disease leaves behind for families and loved ones.

PEACEFUL POINT by Jossine Abrahams

#Peace and Individuality

As the years have gone by, I've learned how to accommodate peace in my life because of so many life lessons in which I had to make peace with others. Peace must have a special meaning that reflects the individuals who have shaken hands on it. Peace must have no arrogance and reveal the remorse of those who have disturbed it from the beginning. For a better life and greater relation-ship with others, peace has to really show in the behaviors, attitudes, and recognition of one's shortcomings, while quickly learning to apologize and forgive each other.

What we should remember, in the process of peace-making, is what's been done wrong and forgive as the Holy Bible says: *"Do unto others as it would be done unto you."* Peace brings harmony and provides a fresh start.

Once we have come to the decision of forgiveness, peace is therefore reflected in the way we communicate to each other. It should be amicably respected for people to move on with life. As human beings, some people may need time to truly forget about what broke the peace. Therefore, it's vital to respect one another and give each other time for healing. People come to terms with things differently. Although peace has been made, healing sometimes is like a wound, so nursing the transformation period is fundamental. It has to be reciprocated, otherwise the healing can be a disappointment if individuals are not patient.

Peace comes within ourselves or from friendly people outwardly showing a smile and positive temperament. Therefore, as we radiate this, we can say to ourselves, "Well done!" and can now give and receive peace and happiness. Peace can be a self-refreshing, habit-forming, positive, mental attitude that others can greatly benefit from. We cannot criticize ourselves or anyone else who wants to be an advocate for peace. As human beings, we chose to seek peace all the time for it reflects love for one another and continued hope.

I have great wisdom and understanding now on how a peaceful environment within us plays a major role in life. I am forever praying for a peaceful world. How I wish the whole planet would value peace, and together we could be one. If only we could work together and achieve one common goal, this world would be a wonderful place to live.

Parents should always pray for their children to discern bad company, and to choose peace. Our wisdom can then become their true wisdom and it will transcend all color, race, and religion.

As one human race, let's all strive for the same goal of peace and happiness.

Born in Africa, Jossine is the CEO of Life Change Home Care Ltd in London, UK since 2014. Her diverse caring skills and knowledge are advanced. She has co-authored in The Depth of Her Soul, an Amazon Best-Seller, is the author of Curse or Blessing Being Spinster being published soon, and is aiming for motivational speaking/coaching.

Facebook: jossine kaizirwe

CHAPTER EIGHT by Karlene Johnson

Finding My Peace through Faith and Fear

My late husband and I met in 1998 while attending high school. Who would have ever thought this boy would become my Prince Charming, end up being my husband, and having seven children with me. I will never forget.

Over the years, my husband worked and would come home exhausted and very fatigued. One day, I noticed he had an extreme amount of weight loss. He was always thirsty and irritable, which wasn't like him. At this point, I was already working from home which gave me more flexibility with our young children. As the days went by, I observed my husband's condition getting worse. He was diagnosed with Graves' disease, which led to his eventual heart failure. I held onto my faith, and started to pray, "Almighty God, thank you for loving me more than I know. Thank you that you allowed me to go through many things that have designed my life for a special purpose. Today, I ask you to fill me with yourself through the power of the Holy spirit. I make myself available for you to use me to bring your hope, love, mercy, and grace to others and especially to those I come in contact with today. I am looking forward to seeing what you will do in and through me. Thank you. Amen."

After he spent five weeks in the hospital, my husband was released. The conversations and prayers we would have always kept us grounded. At times, his faith would become weak and mine as well, but we continued to strengthen each other. My soul of faith always answered to me and said, "Hold on, it's not time yet." I couldn't understand it at the time, but God had a plan. My biggest fear was losing my husband. In 2011, my husband ended up in the hospital once again, but God brought us through it! My husband, myself, and our children continued to focus more on God; there was no place in my home for the enemy of our faith. We had to at all times remember to place all our worries and fears in His hands, and ask Him to give us peace as we faced our days.

Another test. December 2012 was extremely cold with lots of snow. My children would normally wake up and fill my bedroom with laughter and love watching Saturday morning cartoons. That morning was unusually quiet and still, and I woke up early to make breakfast. I kissed my husband and he kissed me back, not knowing that would have been my last kiss with him. By 11 am, my two daughters were getting ready to go Boxing Day shopping. One of the girls went into the bedroom calling her dad, but there no answer. She tickled his foot, but there was no movement. She then screamed, "Mom call 911. Dad's not breathing!" I ran upstairs. To my surprise, my husband was in the same position as I left him when we kissed each other. I got on the bed and touched him. I said, "Wake up!" No movements; no sound. He was cold...so cold. My daughter then performed CPR, but nothing happened. My son tried as well, but the results were the same. My husband was gone.

During this time, one of my most comforting scriptures I held on to, in my time of need, was Deuteronomy 31:6, *"Do not be afraid or terrified because of them, for the Lord your God goes with you, he will never leave you nor forsake you."* My children felt so alone. Every day I would pray with them and for them; I would explain to them that even though their earthly father had left them, their Father in Heaven loved them. I also embraced the story of Job, who lost everything but still held on to God and never let go. We need to learn to lean on God and wait upon him. I told myself and the children that the Lord has given us life and love so we can give love back, wisdom to make us wise with understanding, and a vision to see what the physical eyes cannot see but what the spiritual eyes can. Life after death; I still have life even though a big part of me died...but I'm alive. Yesterday I cried; today I smile with joy. I continue to pray. You have to be able to find the peace within. I had to tell myself I will know peace when...I realize I'm never alone. The loss of my husband was unexpected. In the midst of my great darkness, I made my light shine. God uses us in His master plan to change lives.

With my husbands' passing, we found peace in the comfort of family and the Lord. Without the support and encouragement of family, who knows what our journey would have been like. We all had challenges dealing with our loss, but once we got to the point of acceptance, it all got easier to have peace amongst ourselves knowing he's in a better place. What also helped with engaging in things we enjoyed, whether it was drawing, singing, playing the piano, or just trying new events. It wasn't easy but no one can tell you how long you should grieve. At the same time, you want to enjoy the life you have and be a mentor in someone else's life; everyone has a purpose. Without peace in my life, there would be disorder. When things are out of order, there is chaos and confusion.

I felt secure knowing God is faithful and I held on to that truth, knowing I could count on God. His word settled in my heart and I knew he was present with us. The plan God has for us couldn't change the fear, but the hope built courage and strength into our lives. My children and I knew we had to focus on God, and our fears would melt away. Sometimes it was hard to trust God during our times of uncertainty. Personal experience has shown me a few uncomfortable realities about myself and life. I now surrender to

God and His peace.

Through it all, I have learned to live in faith, not fear, to the point of ultimately finding my peace.

Karlene Ambursley Johnson is an Inspirational Co-author, Entrepreneur, and Speaker, and encourages others to heal by sharing her journey following the death of her sweetheart and husband, Derrick. While taking many steps of faith, it led her to a peace that surpasses all of her understanding. Karlene has helped many women throughout her more than twenty years as a hair-stylist to feel beautiful inside and out by means of her many talents. With her vast knowledge of mental health and wellness issues, she continues to educate the wider community. Karlene has volunteered for years within the Toronto District School Board and lives in Toronto, Ontario with her children.

PEACE IS POWERFUL

CHAPTER NINE by Anita Sechesky

Peace is Powerful

Often times our perspectives of the people in our lives is affected by what's going on inside of us. As sensitive individuals, these relationships play a key role in the way we show up in the world. We identify ourselves, based on the emotional experiences we have lived through, we become a product of our environment. That being said, when we are aware that we cannot change anyone but ourselves, our true peaceful evolution of awareness and enlightenment powerfully evolves. Personal relationships validate our existence, allowing us the freedom to become our very best selves.

Even successful people started somewhere when no one knew who they were, and they probably experienced anxiety, stress, or discouragement. Yet, at the very moment they were going to let it all go, someone offered them kind words of encouragement.

Peace is powerful because it affects every facet of our lives. It's the foundation of how we respond and interact with every person we come in contact with. It causes us to take responsibility for our behaviors because everyone is affected by the words that come out of our mouths. The actions we display towards others is an indication of our mental health and well-being. For instance, if we don't process our experiences and determine the difference between right and wrong, or what's acceptable in our society, our outward behaviors reveal a disruption in our lives. Therefore, our attitudes are projected and can make a difference between forming a friendship or creating an enemy.

A healthy mindset allows us this opportunity to fully comprehend how to establish a balanced life of peace towards everyone we are associated with. Although life has no guarantees, once we learn the various ways to create and find peace, we heal our minds, souls, and bodies. Choosing this way of life will continually attract peace and harmony. Our health improves and our focus is determined. The stresses of life dissipate and we easily recognize the need to be there for others. Stepping outside of our comfort zones, permits us the power to help others find healing, hope, and peace in their lives as well. Developing a habit of peace and gratitude constantly attracts good things into our lives. Relationships that were strained begin to heal and take on new possibilities, allowing for more like-minded individuals to come into our lives.

I encourage you to seriously examine all your relationships within your inner and outer circle. As a Registered Nurse, I have personally observed how traumatic it is when family members lose their loved ones, especially when there are gaps in the communication process and the emotional, spiritual, and physical bond of visiting and being present are broken. Many times, I have seen precious souls leave this world with broken hearts and spirits because of family disputes and disagreements. It's a sad thing to see the look in their eyes, worried if their loved ones will come to see them before their departure. Our lives have no guarantees, but we can make the choices to love and place value where it belongs. Once life is over, there are no second chances as we know of. Love is all there is and all there ever will be when all else is gone. Make peace before it's too late.

Anita Sechesky is a Best-Seller Publisher, Registered Nurse, Certified Professional Coach, NLP and LOA Wealth Practitioner, Best-Seller Consultant, multiple International Best-Selling Author, as well as a Workshop Facilitator and Conference Host. She is the Founder and CEO of Anita Sechesky - Living Without Limitations Inc. and the Founder and Publisher of LWL PUBLISHING HOUSE. Anita was born in Guyana, South America and moved to Canada when she was only four years old. Assisting many people to break through their own limiting beliefs in life and business, Anita had discovered her passion to help individuals release their stories in-to successful publications. She has five Best-Selling books, including four anthologies, in which approximately 200 International authors and co-authors have benefited to date from her expertise. Anita launched her first solo book *"Absolutely You – Overcome False Limitations and Reach Your Full Potential"* in November 2014. As a Best-Seller Publisher, Anita helps people to put their positive perspectives into print.

CHAPTER TEN by Kathie Tuhkanen

A Silent and Peaceful Connection

A crumpled up, poorly folded sheet of paper is handed to me. A name, identification number, and a few items are listed on it and a hopeful stare comes from the young lady holding the page. She's dressed in what she could find earlier that morning, and asks if it's okay for her to look around the store to find what she needs. I try to help her find the sizes of clothing listed on the voucher. She isn't really sure what to think as I help her through the racks of clothing. I pull many different garments down off the racks and pile up her small cart until it's difficult to maneuver. I encourage her to take the basket to the dressing room to make sure the clothing will actually fit. Her awkward hesitation says it all. I've seen this situation time and time again.

I don't know her particular story, but like many before her, she had a life established somewhere. However, her circumstances changed and things started to go bad. She might have lost her job, it could have been the loss of a loved one, or some other event that triggered the dramatic shift in her life. Things have certainly not been the same again afterwards, but it never is. She may have suddenly fled through the middle of the night with only the clothes on her back and a small bag she had hidden away with a friend for safe keeping. I'll never really know where she was coming from, but wherever she was going, I was going to be the one to help her at the beginning of that journey.

She pulled the curtain across the dressing room and made sure several times that the curtain was fully across the doorway so that no one could see her as she tried on the clothes. I tried to busy myself and I would occasionally go to the curtain and call into the room, "How are you doing in there?" to which I would only have a quiet reply, "Okay...I think."

After asking her for permission, I would move the curtain slightly so that only I could see into the small room and glimpse this shadow of a person standing in front of the mirror, gazing up and down the mirror in expressionless disbelief, either at the outfit or at her reflection, she wonders, "How did it get so far?"

Outfit after outfit, she stands there and looks vacantly at the image in the mirror. I hear her as she stops moving, then stares after trying on each ensemble. I pull the curtain aside and peak in to find her standing motionless for a few moments before turning and letting me know she will try on the next articles in the stack of clothing.

Finally nearing the end of the pile, I look in and see tears streaming down her blank face. As much as I wanted to hug her, I didn't know her other than as a broken soul. I lightly placed my hand on her shoulder and my touch is just enough to cause sobs to emanate from the pain deep within, past the point of numbness, loneliness, and desolation.

After a long hug and numerous shed tears, a few concerned people wondering how things were for us, I was able to get our mystery lady to finish trying on her few remaining articles of clothing. A few people were near the dressing room once she emerged from behind the curtain; she looked down and made her way past them without saying a word.

I found her again at the clothing racks, trying to put most of the clothes away. She only kept a fraction of what I had gotten for her. I quietly helped her and we again looked at a few more garments so that she could possibly find enough to help her through the next few days. Neither of us said a word to each other for quite some time. We would just glance at each other.

We only were able to find a few more item, but I could tell from her body language she didn't want to try them on. I could hear her stomach gurgling, the way she hunched when it made noises, and how she occasionally wiped the side of her mouth, I could tell she quite possibly hadn't eaten in at least a day, maybe longer.

It was now time to process her voucher. As the cashier tallied up the bill, the young lady's eyes intently watched the charges add up. The moment she saw her total, I thought she was going to burst into tears again. Her faced was flushed red, she started to sweat, and I could see she was about to panic. The cashier pressed a series of buttons and the total was...zero. The sigh of relief was deafening.

She thanked us for the help and was about to leave when I asked her to follow me to the back lunch room. Earlier in the day, a tray of sweet treats was dropped off by a regular customer, and some of the volunteers had brought in savory bite-sized snacks. I invited her to sit with me and enjoy the delectable bounty. She carefully chose one small piece and slowly savored the tiny mouthful for what seemed an abnormally long time. Motioning to her to have another, she pondered which piece to have next, and then thoroughly savored it. Repeatedly, she was encouraged to take piece after piece until she had finished most of the first plate. By now, she was starting to talk a little between mouthfuls. We each enjoyed our cup of coffee and though she revealed little about her past, I did find out she was starting over again. She was currently staying wherever she could to keep off the streets. She had friends in the area and was able to take them up on their offers of kindness, staying on one couch for a few days before moving on to the next. All her possessions fit in a small backpack which she carried with her everywhere as she didn't know for sure where her head would lay later that night.

She was quite mature for her age and while we chatted, I could sense that she wanted to have a more permanent housing solution. We discussed various situations and agreed upon the best solution. Phone calls were made and meetings were setup over the next two days. Afterwards, her emotions overwhelmed her as she wept again, this time for the extra efforts being made on her behalf. Imagine, she came to the store hoping to find something that she could wear, and instead she was able to find healing through the tears that were shared during such a difficult time. Our young mystery lady had walked in, desolate and demoralized, trying to avoid contact with anyone, but over the course of nearly two hours, she started to open up and accept the help that she truly was in need of. This allowed a sense of peace and solitude to come upon her.

She left the store shortly afterwards with her small backpack in hand. I felt good letting her leave, because I knew that things were in place for her to start a new journey in life. I had helped fuel her body and soul with care and compassion. She was able to find, in that tiny thrift store, what was missing in her life until that very moment. She found peace.

We never did see her again. I don't know for sure if she made it to the appointments that were arranged for her, but the peaceful look in her eyes as she thanked the cashier and I will forever be etched in my memories.

Kathie Tuhkanen is a Health & Wellness Life Coach and a Business Consultant specializing in nutrition and financial planning. She is very involved in the non-profit sector, offering various forms of support. Kathie is a loving mother, engaged in the local community, and making this world a better place.

Email: Kathiej@live.ca

PEACEFUL POINT by Mary Hilty

#Peace is a Name to Live "Up To"

My name is Peace and I come from this amazing family of very busy members. I have sisters named Faith, Hope, and Charity and I have brothers named Humility, Gratitude, and my oldest brother, Humanity. We are a closely bound family of "do-gooders" and thankfully each of us has the ability to participate and motivate all of the other family members.

Dinners in our home are lively and filled with encouragement and discussion about who will do what and who will play what role today. We all stay very busy and at times we have to do our part without much help from our other family members. Thankfully, all of us depend upon the others and none of us ever mind being helpful for the challenges which lie ahead.

My sisters and brothers tell me that right now in our time, and in our world, I have a whole lot to do. I am invited to big dinners, to other countries, and I am often the guest of honor at these events. It seems that everybody wants me to be present, but there are times when getting me to those places is very difficult. I always have a deep desire to be where I am invited and I always bring the best of myself wherever I go. There are times when the places I visit are not quite certain what they can do with me and I must make my intentions very clear. Being Peace, you see, comes with enormous responsibility. Most of the time Faith, Charity, and Hope will tag along and we find that together we begin to make those places we visit a whole lot happier and improved. These are the visits we all enjoy the most and closes the doors to all of the meetings. And Humanity...ahh, Humanity seems to be the benefactor of everything that is discussed and shared in these meetings. It is important to know that Humanity does not need to attend these meetings, wherever on Earth they are held. I am told that it is completely normal for Humanity to eat dinner in our home with all of the brothers and sisters while simultaneously sharing meals with other families and friends throughout the world. I have always known that Humility would make it easier for me to accept that my contribution as Peace was mostly to make Humanity stronger and better.

Our "family" travels the world, visits every home, hospital, and clinic. We visit every war zone, every conference, and we sit down at the tables of great visionaries and dignitaries the world over. We are a part of every movement, every family, every community...every government. We are at the beginning and the end of everything that mattered yesterday and today, and everything that will ever matter. I am Peace and I do not come alone. I have Faith, Hope, Charity, Humility, Gratitude, and Humanity along with me wherever and whenever I travel. And guess what else? We are all direct descendants of LOVE. Amazing family!

Mary Hilty has written extensively through journaling, composing poems, and a variety of articles. She considers her social interactions with people to be one of her greatest inspiration for writing, which she has been doing most of her life. A favorite dream is to co-create with other authors and leave her "best self" in the world through writing!

CHAPTER ELEVEN by Leah Lucas

Surviving Life's Losses with the Peace of God

There comes a time in everyone's life when an event or situation becomes so overwhelming or intense that you start to question your faith in the Lord. Even if you have no faith in Him at that time, questions arise in one's troubled mind such as: "Who am I?", "Why am I here?", "What is my purpose in life?", or the most difficult for me that I never found the answer to, "How can I bare all that is happening to me in this life without going crazy or falling to the darkness?"

I found myself asking these questions repeatedly every single day to the point where I honestly thought that there was no way out of my gloom. I had been continually crying for a few days and nights. I had sought out the help of a counselor who told me a number of times that all I needed to do was take a deep breath and everything would be okay (I threw a chair in her office). I was very much not okay. On my way home from that doctor's office, while gripping my steering wheel to the point of having white knuckles, I held back the most disturbing thoughts of my demise. I didn't have an accident or run my car off the bridge I had to drive over to get home. I made it back to my place. Thank God!

I was going through my divorce that was brutal and devastating, on every level that one never wishes to reach. My children were taken away from me at one point. I was struggling to stay clean after a few rehabs. I was feeling scared, alone, and deeply saddened.

One day I prayed to God, crying out loud to give me the strength to go on. I begged Him to give me the courage I needed to get through my days ahead because I truly felt as if I just couldn't live another day feeling so trapped and isolated inside myself. God answered my prayer that day and it was the beginning of my true faith in the Lord. Since then, I have never had another negative thought of that nature again. I know I will never again reach that point because my faith in God is always there. He is continually with me, and never leaves me in my times of need.

I realize that for me, there was a series of certain, specific events that led me down the path to doubt my faith, and question if my beliefs were strong enough to stand the test of time and trust in God to lead the way. A few key things occurred that I feel confidently in my heart happened intentionally because God himself sent these signs for me to see. From then on, I trusted completely in the Lord. I knew that even though my life was not going to be easy, I knew that God was with me and I could handle anything life chose to challenge me with.

I now look back on past events and sometimes I cry. My Life decided to challenge me starting in April of 2014. I had just been evicted from my apartment and was relocating to Everett, WA, to share a rental house with someone I knew from high school. The place was not great, but…I had to leave the last place and had no other options. I moved into this house and told everyone I knew that this was going to be the very beginning of the rest of my life. I was all on my own and felt proud for probably a week. Then suddenly I fell into another period of darkness within my heart and mind. I was lost, angry, and fighting with, it seemed at the time, every human being on the planet. Face-to-face, by phone, text, or online, I was just raging mad. Yelling at everyone and doing nothing but blaming everyone else for my complete misery, I spent hours on end crying my eyes out. It was at that time I decided I would lean into my faith completely. I trusted God and knew if I just spent the time praying with all my heart and followed His word and His path for me, I'd end up in a better place. So I shut off my phone, blocked myself from any social media, just sat on my bed, read my bible, prayed, and wrote letters to God and to my grandmother who had passed away. I sat there for about three weeks, just being one with the Lord. I can honestly say that I walked outside after that time, feeling whole. That was the second week in May 2014. I carried on with my life.

It was Memorial Day weekend, May 24th, 2014. I was supposed to have my two kids with me that weekend, but instead I asked my ex-husband to look after them. I felt I needed a mental break. The kids stayed with their dad that weekend and I'm so happy that they did. I was visiting a friend of mine in Issaquah for the weekend. It was about 5:30 am Saturday morning when my friend, who lived on the other side of my house (it was divided into a duplex) called me. I asked her why she was calling so early since it was a holiday weekend. Right then, I heard in her voice that something was terribly wrong. She told me that a fire had broken out in our house and I needed to get up there right away. I thought she was joking; I really did. She said to me, "Leah, get up here now! There's been a fire here and the fire marshal is telling me that your side of the house is a total loss!"

I dropped my phone and went down on my knees. I was screaming and crying, saying out loud, "No, no, no! God, you said you would always be with me and protect us from harmful things. Now this happens? You let my house burn down?" I didn't know what to think or how to feel. I couldn't even speak words for about five hours. My friend drove my car back to my house because I was obviously in no shape to drive. We arrived to see fire trucks everywhere. People were still standing around watching the firefighters dig for hot spots. A few police officers were taking statements from anyone who happened to witness the fire as it started. Honestly, after seeing the black, burnt outside of the house as we pulled up, I just fell out of my car to the ground. I was weak from overwhelming feelings of "Oh my God, this is not happening to me right now." With my friend's help, I slowly walked up to the house and in an instant, I fell to my hands and knees in the burnt ashes with water still spilling out of hoses next to me. I was paralyzed. No feelings or emotions at all. I was completely numb, yet I was crying helplessly, just kneeling there. Staring at my burnt home, I was in shock. It was all I could do in that moment – crying in the ashes that were my entire life. All of it was just...gone. Everything. I suddenly screamed out, "Noooo, where are Punkie Pie and Lilly Cakes...? Where are my ten-month-old kittens? Please someone, anyone, tell me they got out!" The fireman just looked at me, then looked to the ground, apologized, and walked away. My two kittens that my kids and I had rescued over the summer were gone too.

I have never in my life felt such utter deep sadness. It was truly soul-crushing. One minute I had a life and all these items that I had saved and earned and kept my entire lifetime. Now, in the blink of my eyes, it was gone. Everything. All I had ever known, worked for, built, and saved in my lifetime. Ashes. Burnt, black, smelly, water-damaged... beyond saving anything. What was I going to do? I was consumed with endless thoughts and questions about "What happens to me now?" That fire took all my earthly possessions. All of it. I had nothing left: my schooling, my cleaning business that I had started all on my own the previous winter, our poor kittens. All I could do was cry.

A few minutes later, even though to me it felt like I had been kneeling there for eternity, a gentleman from the Red Cross walked over to me, helped to pick me up off the ground and out of the ashes and water. I don't even know how long he stood there asking me questions, but to this day I can't tell you what he was saying. I heard nothing. The man helped me into a mobile crisis unit van and thank God my friend was there with me. I couldn't even tell the guy my name. I just sat there, asking God, "How could you do this to me and my family?" Finally, after about an hour, I came to. We went over some papers and found a hotel for me to stay in for the next few days. The Red Cross worker gave me a voucher for food and one for some clothing. He tried to assure me I was going be okay because the insurance would pay for the losses and I'd be just fine. It would just take time to process the claim and issue me a check. I told him that I didn't have renter's insurance because I was only staying for five weeks, and was set to move out in just two weeks' time. I had no way to recover from this. The guy looked at me and said he was sorry for our devastating loss. Then he grabbed my hands, held them in his, and prayed for us. His first words were, "Thank you Lord for sparing all the lives that you did today. We are so blessed and thankful that this family was not home this morning and that the other family was able to make it to safety. We ask now Lord that you take these two families into your arms and love and shelter them through the next for weeks while they rebuild their lives." I was now falling over onto this man and crying. It was all I could do. I thanked everyone for their help and then asked my friend to drive me to my hotel.

As I laid on the bed and cried, I was shivering and shaking, not from being cold, but because my body had no idea how to handle the amount of emotions that were running through me during these first twenty-four hours. I just sobbed and let the endless streams of tears roll down my face.

My daughter was at a school camp all that week. So when she came back three days after the fire had occurred, my ex-husband asked that I wait to tell our son until his sister was home. He wanted them to be together when I told them this awful news. My stomach just ached non-stop knowing that the very first question from my kids was going to be, "Did Punkie and Lilly make it out? Are they alive?" I just didn't want to be the one to give them that kind heartache and sadness – while they were off having fun at camp, their kittens and all their belongings burned in a fire, and now they had nothing with mom anymore. They're my children, so small and innocent, and no child should have to endure this kind of tragic loss. I wasn't even sure how to tell them.

I met the kids at their dad's house after they had settled in from camp. We all sat on the back deck, and as soon as my son saw me, he knew something was very wrong. He said nothing to me, just ran over and hugged my waist. I started crying instantly. We sat them down and I told them what had happened. My daughter turned and buried her face into her father's chest and he held her while she cried. All she could say was, "Poor Punkie and Lilly." My son's eyes went from scared to a deep sadness that just over-whelmed me in an instant. But he did not cry. He hugged me, and wrapped his arms around my neck and did not let go. Telling my kids about the fire was the hardest thing I have ever had to do in my life. We cried together as a family and then I left them with their dad that night.

We still say the same thing when I tuck him in at night. He starts by saying, "I love you." And I say, "I love you more." Then he says back, "No Mom, I love you most!" I hug him so tight, pray, and thank God for giving me the best, most understanding two children any mom could ever ask to be blessed with. These precious moments are what bring peaceful balance into my life.

Through this entire life-altering event that left me homeless for that summer, I never once questioned my faith in the Lord. When I said that prayer a few years back when I was ready to end it all, I gave my will over to God. That is how I found and kept my peace within my faith. Whatever it is in life that is too much for me to bear, I pray and send it up to God, and he takes over. He died for our sins and takes our burdens away when it's too much for us. Without my undying faith and trust in the Lord, I would not be alive today, nor would I experience the peace within myself that I do every day.

That's how powerful peace the Lord's peace has been for me.

Leah Lucas is a single mother of two amazing kids. She works for a leading Property Management company and is studying at Bellevue College for her AA in Business Management in Real Estate. Leah is an inspiration to all around her. She has fought to become who she is today after hitting rock bottom in her own life. Her smile and outgoing personality makes her great company. Her quirky humor and point of views allow her to see things from different angles. Leah is a caring, intelligent, and peace-loving woman who has gained wisdom through life experience. She enjoys work and her family.

CHAPTER TWELVE by Ruth Farvardin

Reflections of Peace through the Years

Then we contemplate peace, what do we think of? Freedom from worry? Prosperity? Good health? Liberty to move about freely? Happy relationships? All of these are pleasant, yet many have found peace in chains or in circumstances that most of us would consider to be very unwelcome. Mankind has been, throughout recorded history, on an eternal quest for peace. Many centuries ago it was written that man would cry for peace, but there would be none. Today, as we so often wake up to news of another violent or disturbing event that has taken place, that prophesy may certainly seem accurate.

How do we, either individually or collectively, achieve thus illusive state called peace? How can we find harmony in the midst of so much confusion? Civilizations and individuals alike have been searching and writing about it from time immemorial. It has been written that the Maker of the universe is not the author of confusion, but rather of peace, so where do we look for answers? Where does peace start? Mother Theresa wrote, *"Peace begins with a smile."* She also wrote, *"The fruit of service is peace."* Practically echoing this are the words of a familiar song written by Sy Miller and Jill Jackson, *"Let There Be Peace On Earth and Let It Begin With Me."*

None of us live in a vacuum. Everything that we are is a part of and is affected by everything around us. Science is only beginning to fathom the complexity of our existence. Yet some things remain simple, like the predictable smile that most humans display in response to the smile and voice of a baby. Each of us resonates throughout the universe, just like our minds are connected to the hands that have the ability to reach out to others, and feet that we can set on a path that can make a difference for good, for anything that we are destined to touch. If mankind would, instead of trying to defy the laws that govern nature, rather endeavor to work with and learn from nature, we almost inevitably would live longer and more peaceful lives. I believe we are here to learn peace that comes from aligning ourselves with the same laws that govern the orbit of the earth and the universal elements in their circuits.

John F. Kennedy stated well when he said, "Mankind must put an end to war, or war will put an end to mankind." With all of the violence and confusion reigning in the world today, the question that begs to be answered, literally, is "What are we thinking?" The key to answering that question is not in either beating ourselves up or patting ourselves on the back, but rather in examining our focus! Where are our thoughts taking us? It has been said that "what we think about, we bring about." We naturally gravitate toward that which we most desire, either consciously or unconsciously. If we don't see peace within ourselves or our world, it may be advantageous to take stock of our thoughts.

Einstein once wrote, *"Peace cannot be kept by force; it can only be achieved by understanding."* If peace begins with "me", a good place to start is by understanding ourselves and focusing on "what we are thinking." The best way to change the direction of a vehicle is by turning the steering wheel, which in this case can be likened to our thoughts changing the direction of our footsteps. It is written, *"As a man thinks, so he is."* If we think thoughts of harmony, gratitude, and service, this helps to turn the direction of our environment around us, and ultimately the universe of which we are a part of. We are only just beginning to fathom the intricacies of our relationship with the elements around us, large and small. With the understanding that Einstein spoke of, our eyes can be reopened to see and hear, with a new heart, the beauty and songs of nature.

Wise men have told us to think on good things like love, joy, peace, truth, honesty, and things that are pure and lovely. There is no law against these. They can only lift the heart and renew the spirit. One can think of harmony as all of these good things combining together on an instrument to make beautiful music.

Like it or not, however, in this life there are always conflicts within and without. Our attitude and perspective in seeing these conflicts determines much of our peace. Many people react to obstacles with great stress and negativity. Others respond to unpleasant events by learning how to achieve harmony through service and forgiveness. Peace is not the absence of conflicts or distractions from life's difficulties or losses, but comes from persevering and growing strong in the face of them. Pay attention to the immutable laws of nature, noting how the trees that survive bend, but also spring back.

Unexpected circumstances are inevitable in life and depending on one's outlook, can be considered as positive or negative – the proverbial glass half-full or glass half-empty. To be truthful, obstacles are a necessary part of growth, both in nature and in character building. A plant that meets no resistance from wind or weather grows weak and shallow rooted. The herbs and trees that grow under harsh conditions send taproots deep into the soil to avail themselves of the nutrients they need to survive and are more medicinally valuable. We too, when we meet difficult circumstances, need to dig deep within ourselves to search for strength and inner resources.

Eleanor Roosevelt wisely joked that "A woman is like a teabag; you can't tell how strong she is until you put her in hot water."

Even nature's reactions involve positive and negative charges. Taking lessons from nature, we learn that the plants and animals that survive aren't necessarily the strongest, but are rather the most flexible and adaptable. It's wise to be flexible and understanding with others by celebrating the different perspectives and unique qualities that they can contribute, and in the same way serve to build peace within and without.

Ultimately, to achieve real peace, we need to take stock of what we really want and why. If we just want to have something to please or impress someone else, we are only hurting ourselves, and perhaps those we are trying to please also. Many of the world's conflicts today have their roots in ego building, even on national and world levels. Until we recognize the importance and urgency of a goal that is worthy to accomplish, there is a tendency for human nature to procrastinate until a crisis point has been reached. It is said that Albert Einstein was asked, "What do you think of the Third World War?" Reportedly, he answered, "I don't know about the Third World War, but I will tell you about the Fourth. When you go to wage the Fourth World War, it will be with sticks and bows and arrows. We will be back to primitive man."

As previously stated, we gravitate toward what is, ultimately, important to us, which is why it is important to recognize the possible consequences of our actions. There are natural laws that operate like gravity and produce either peace or conflicts. These principles produce pain when disregarded, and peace when respected. Treat others, and do business with others, as you would like to have them treat you and your family. If these laws aren't respected, peace is an illusion and will never last.

Many lose hope that lasting peace will ever be. However, I have high hopes for ultimate peace. In nature, you see many parallels that correspond with life. You can look at the seasons and see that they go through their changes and are renewed. Nature is not without conflict, but after the night is past, the sun rises, the light illuminates the earth and warms us again. The songbirds return from their journey, the trees bud and grow, new leaves appear, and there is revitalization. The winter ground awakens from its rest and the earth becomes fruitful again. We see that the earth keeps turning on its axis; the sun, the moon, and the planets keep to their prescribed and allotted pathways, as science develops more and more sophisticated instruments that allow us to observe. I don't accept that these things happen by accident. I believe that the harmony, the order, and precision of the laws that govern and define the universe bespeak of an underlying purpose. Through this hope, my "Peace is Perfected."

Ruth Farvardin lives in eastern Washington state, (USA), with her adult, autistic daughter. Most recently, Ruth was a coauthor in an anthology compiled by Anita Sechesky, published by LWL PUBLISHING HOUSE, and entitled *"#LOVE - A New Generation Of Hope Continues..."* Ruth has spent most of her working life in holistic health, and continues to encourage the use of medicinal plants and methods of healing which produce harmony, both within ourselves and in our relationship to our universe. Ruth also finds enjoyment and peace in gardening, photography, painting, and in researching the continuing developments in holistic healing and nutritional science.

PEACEFUL POINT by Marigrace Galura

#Peace is Being Present

Peace is important in my life, and a choice that I make. I can remember times where I felt only a few good days. The rest of time was stressful. I felt hopeless. A breakthrough happened when I took yoga lessons. It had started towards the end of the class when it was time to meditate. I was in a corpse pose and encouraged to breathe deeply in and out. Then I noticed the changes within myself. I felt better and at peace. This was a success and really made a difference.

In class, we focused on our breathing and being in the present moment. Peace showed up for me – no worries or busy thoughts. I continued the breathing techniques when I needed to relax. It was a tool necessary for my peace of mind.

Some actions for peace that work for me are saying prayers with healing intentions. Reciting positive affirmations of peace give me a relaxed state – believing things will work out on their own. When I create jewelry, I feel peace as well. My mind is relaxed and ready to inspire more creativity.

I attended a retreat during one weekend, which was a special time to just be me and connect with like-minded women. My intention was to get some clarity from within. I participated in activities where I got to reflect on my immediate thoughts, without judgment. My senses were indulged with tasting healthy luscious food. I smelled wonderful scents through essential oils, practiced yoga, meditated, and was surrounded with positive people who were nurturing. I couldn't help but feel relaxed after the end of the day. I was at peace and felt the love from within. My cup was full and ready to share.

What is peace to me? It's feeling calm and having a sense of harmony around my world. I have discovered visualization through taking workshops. With visualization, I am able to achieve a sense of peace from within. There are pleasant things, environments, and feelings I have visualized. In reality, I can go to the beach, watch the cool water, and hear the waves going through. A walk amongst nature gives me a sense of peace. Staying in the present moment and being accepting of a situation is effective. Something as simple as being aware of your breathing evokes peace. One of the most important things that works for me is self-acceptance. It made me happier from within. I no longer pressure myself to overachieve and realize that I am enough. People have noticed that I have a peaceful demeanor. I am in the present moment ready to accept whatever happens in my life. I believe in the higher being like God to help me feel at peace. I know with him I can almost handle anything. There have been miracles I recognized in my daily life and feeling peace is one of them. I can achieve anything I set my mind to with peace and it is powerful.

Marigrace is a Fashion Accessories Artist and designer who handcrafts jewelry with insight to peoples' personalities. Her goals are to have others express themselves creatively and ignite their unique personal style. Marigrace enjoys empowering others through storytelling and sharing experiences.

Social Media: https://www.facebook.com/Marigrace AccessoriesInc

CHAPTER THIRTEEN by Darla Ouellette

Let Your Peace Shine

Peace can be defined in many different ways. Some people find peace through being quiet and still – meditating and relaxing. Others find tranquility doing what they love – helping others, and having faith and gratitude. Peace can be found in a multitude of places. Mind, body, and Spirit are all connected, however, each can have harmony within separately.

Peace is a choice. It's either something people already possess, or are seeking to find. When we choose to live a life of harmony and create that harmonious life for ourselves, we create peace for others around us. Peace is not always easy to find or achieve. Peace can be difficult to maintain. It needs to be polished like a rare diamond or piece of fine jewelry. It quite often needs to be fine-tuned and kept moving and flowing through us. In order to do this, we must be realistic. We are all going to have days where the weight of the world catches up with us. So how do we learn to keep this diamond shining bright within us? So bright it casts a brilliant glow for all those around us? For myself, I have learned that having faith and gratitude are very important. Without those qualities, we become cynical and jaded. We let the worldly stress-es erode our peace and give our power away. So many times in life we have unexpected mishaps, major tragedies, accidents, financial woes, and even the stresses of daily living. So how do we overcome all of these things? I believe it is how we've learned to handle these difficult situations that get us back to that inner peace and harmonious life balance. Like so many people in life, I myself have had many struggles and have overcome many adversities along the way. It hasn't been easy and some days are better than others. What keeps me motivated to reconnect with that inner peace is knowing the joy it will bring to me and the people who surround me. The satisfaction, and calming sensation that comes over you when you have achieved your inner peace and are able to see the world with a whole new perspective, renews your faith in humanity and makes you feel refreshed and awakened to the possibilities that lie ahead. It allows you to dream, reach for the stars, and realize that it will all be okay and work out. Good things are coming. You will shine bright again, even if you are struggling to find your peace right now. You will find it again.

What follows are few things that I believe are essential to letting peace shine in your life:

1) Have faith and gratitude.

Believe in God and the Universe. Believe all will be taken care of as it should be. All will unfold how it is meant to be. We may not like or understand the plan and feel it's unfair, but it is happening for a reason. It's usually a lesson for us to learn to help us grow and blossom into even more divine human spirits. We were created as spiritual beings. Most of us find ourselves, at some point in our lives, searching for answers. Maybe there are no right or wrong answers though. Maybe we are meant to live our lives with joy, happiness, and laughter, and let everything else just "happen." I believe we are meant to have faith in a higher being. For me, that is God and the Universe. I also believe that God lives within all of us. He made us in his likeness and we are all unique, flawed, and yet perfect just the way we are.

2) Don't be so hard on yourself!

You're human and are going to mess some things up along the way. You will make "mistakes" throughout your life. These are actually called life lessons and teach us great and powerful things if we are open and ready to receive these lessons. When we make "mistakes" or "fail," quite often it doesn't end in horrific events taking place, generally speaking. When we do make a "mistake" or "fail" at something, it is really just another opportunity to experience something new and different. It's a chance to change things, create something new, or explore other options.

3) Let it go!

If something is stressing you out and taking away your inner peace, stop and ask yourself these questions: Is this a life and death situation? Is this really as bad as it appears in my mind? Can I survive this? What is the worst thing that can happen? It takes a while but as you play these questions through your mind, you begin to realize that the situation is often not as big or devastating as it seems. Sometimes, there are bigger issues and they are real, scary, and possibly life-threatening. But if you have the tools to know how to handle the smaller stresses, it will strengthen you and empower you to be ready for anything!

4) Let your light shine!

> Love yourself completely and wholly. Love every part of you. You're like a diamond in the rough. You may just need some polishing to make your peace shine bright. Make your edges smooth, learn, and grow into the magnificent wonder that you are. Love those within in your inner circle, your family, and your most valued friends. Show them your inner peace and light and let yourself shine in greatness... in good times and in bad times. Let yourself be the best you that you can be: imperfect and flawed, raw and real, genuine and true to who you are. After all, you cannot become a brilliant diamond without polishing yourself and working on the rough edges. We are not designed to be perfect. Like a diamond, we are all flawed in different ways but unique and special all the same. The best type of diamond to be is a genuine one and live with your light, positivity, and peace shining through you. You'll start to attract others into your inner peace and light. You will be an example for them, showing them how to attract good things into their lives and find their own inner peace.

5) Stay connected with your body.

> Listen to your body and what it needs. The mind, body, and spirit are all connected. Moving your body allows positive energy to flow through you completely and releases natural good-feeling hormones called endorphins throughout your body. Meditation, yoga, walking, and movement are important aspects of what our bodies were made to do. Allow yourself to experiment with what resonates and feels good for you. Permit yourself to try new types of movement and exercise. I have found great relief from pain by increasing my motion, and going for walks with my son, my dog, and friends. You don't even have to join a gym or spend money to create more body movement for yourself.

6) If you get off track, don't give up!

> You can find your peace and light again. Polish that diamond and get smooth and shining again! Make your inner diamond a beacon of light for others to see. Find joy and peace in the little things. Discover those brief moments of peace within your day. Soon those brief points of time will turn into days and weeks. You will start to feel your light, energy, and peace flow into your life naturally. It really is a matter of redirecting, focusing, and taking your power and peace back. Acknowledging where you lost track of your serenity is important. So many of us believe that we must correct our actions immediately and punish ourselves for messing up. Well, life is messy,

hard, and overwhelming, but life is also a blessing and a gift every day when you wake up and take a breath. Each day you get to spend time with your loved ones and friends.

I anticipate these tips have helped you even just slightly by shifting your mindset and opening yourself up to new ways of thinking and possibilities. Be kind to yourself and love yourself deeply. Accept your life's "mistakes" as they become lessons and continue to learn and grow from them. Allow your light to shine and be the best diamond you can be. Live your life with authenticity, kindness, love, and positivity. Do these things and I promise that your own inner light and peace will shine through. It will radiant from deep within you. It will shine to all those around you: your cherished loved ones, family, and friends. Let your peace shine bright!

Darla Ouellette is an accomplished Registered Nurse with over twelve years' experience in various skill settings. She is a Law Of Attraction Life Coach, a published author, and holds two other diplomas for RPN and Law and Security Administration. Darla has always enjoyed writing and finds it very rewarding. She first started composing in Literary publications and authoring poems as well when in High School. Darla is a single mom to her wonderful teenage son Cameron, currently resides in her hometown of Wallaceburg, Ontario, and is working as a Registered Nurse.

PEACEFUL POINT by Jossine Abrahams

#Peace, Perfect Peace

Peace is the result of a healthy reconciliation between different parties involved in a misunderstanding. Our bodies, minds, and souls should be able to accumulate the clear concept of a transformed mind-set to allow individuals to feel at peace. It is in this moment, when one chooses to forgive and forget, that fresh thoughts allow a person to be released from the stressful situations.

Peace is meant to be renewed, clear, clean, and tranquil. It's an inner feeling that can be expressed as an out of body experience, just like every month when we have a new moon that gives us an opportunity to begin again. The question is: are we for forgiveness? For me, the same thought applies to us once we've been hurt. It's vital that we forgive and also apologize to have peace so we can release ourselves from anger, resentment, frustration, hurt, and even grief.

People need to be grateful for the tranquility found in Mother Nature to gather themselves together. Visiting places like Victoria Falls in my homeland of Zimbabwe or Niagara Falls in Canada will help anyone to find peace and serenity. As we appreciate the sun, moon, stars, and fantastic sunsets, we feel a great sense of satisfaction. Seeking relaxation after any kind of strife offers inner peace.

Practicing meditation, exercise, a healthy diet, the outdoors, and taking a much-needed holiday now and again can steer anyone towards a peaceful pathway in life. Let's attempt to move in this direction for the benefits are worthy and healthy to achieve. When you arrive at your peaceful destination, take a moment and observe your surroundings. It's worth listening to the sounds of water flowing or birds singing in the early daylight or at a beautiful sunset. Choosing to seek paradise experiences like that of Trinidad and Tobago, Africa, of the Isle of Wright in England will give you a greater sense of gratitude for our beautiful world.

Choosing a life of peace is fundamentally important because we all experience pain and deceitfulness. Avoiding individuals who create stress can be difficult at times because they may be a close family member or a colleague at work. These experiences are not healthy and can affect one's health and blood pressure, causing confusion, forgetfulness, and if prolonged, more serious health problems. People will always be who they are. We cannot prevent them from gossiping or putting one another down. It's up to each individual to choose what's best for a healthy relationship. Dialogue between the two conflicting parties sometimes helps, however, once there's an awareness that the relationship would be destroyed by further communication, then sometimes the best way is to move on, forgive and forget. This may be the most difficult thing to do, but it helps one to have a better relationship in the long term and to find peace.

Born in Africa, Jossine is the CEO of Life Change Home Care Ltd in London, UK since 2014. Her diverse caring skills and knowledge are advanced. She has co-authored in *The Depth of Her Soul*, an Amazon Best-Seller, is the author of *Curse or Blessing Being Spinster* being published soon, and is aiming for motivational speaking/coaching.

Facebook: jossine kaizirwe

CHAPTER FOURTEEN by Susan Kern

In Search of My Peaceful Connection

All too familiar in our daily lives are the seemingly endless demands and the stressors that accompany them. We have been conditioned to see this way of life as normal and "just the way it is." We work hard to attain our goals and achieve the desired results, and if we do so, we are considered successful. Yet, all too often, this leaves us feeling unfulfilled and generally burnt out. What is missing? How can we change what seems unchangeable? When did we lose sight of ourselves in the pursuit of life?

These were questions I asked of myself so often that I sounded like a broken record in my own mind; and was still without good answers. So dissatisfying had life become that nothing really made sense anymore. It was then that I began asking some new questions, like: "Why am I doing this thing that leaves me feeling depleted and empty?" and "Who said this is how I am supposed to live?"

Well, what was missing? A sense of connection to myself. How could I change what seemed unchangeable? I suppose that was dependent on me believing it to be unchangeable. Maybe I could change my mind on that? Hmm, that might be possible. When did I lose sight of myself? So long ago that I do not recall. Why am I doing things that leave me feeling like crap? Maybe I think that's how I'm supposed to feel. Who said this is how life is? Again, I have no idea. I guess I learned it from watching my family, friends, and coworkers. At times it seems like we compete for who is suffering the most.

At no point in that life is there a moment of peace. Ah, peace; the elusive state that the online Cambridge English dictionary defines as *"freedom from war and violence."* On a global level it is clear that there is little peace within, and between, nations. On a personal level it gets interesting to apply this same definition, freedom from war and violence. "What? That makes no sense," you may say. Let's take a deeper dive into this...

I have long observed myself and others and our continuous struggles to do it all, and be our best. When we fall short of the expectations we set, or others set for us, we have a tendency to judge ourselves as not being good enough. Could that judgment be akin to war or violence, against ourselves? In a symbolic way I believe it is. This was the question that began to dismantle life as I had known it.

To begin, what were the things I was doing (or thinking, or feeling) every day that did not leave me feeling good? Certainly some of those things seemed out of my control, like going to work, yet some of them, like eating junk food and being tired from staying up late and getting up early, were clearly under my power to change, if I chose to empower myself to do so. Just noticing these things was a huge eye opener for me. It didn't require me to change anything; just to notice. I wrote a list of what they were and then pondered what I was willing to let go of and what I still felt attached to. It was easier for me to begin to see the effects of these previously unconscious choices when I was simply noticing. It was somehow...safe.

The exercise of raising my awareness of what was creating self-judgment within me was big. How often did I call myself a loser? Stupid? Ugly? Prior to this I had felt helpless and like a victim in a stressed out world. Seeing what I could change, if I wanted to, made me feel stronger and less victimized. I was actually becoming a player in my life!

The next step was to do one of two things: either (1) make changes and feel better, or (2) decide not to make any changes and to stop judging myself for what I was doing. Over the years I have employed both strategies with variable outcomes. Some changes involve letting go of habits or activities that we never really knew why we did them in the first place. We may not have enjoyed them or just did them because it was easy; maybe friends shared these and it was just "what you do." In my experience, these are the easiest to release. The things we do that are in fact harmful, like eating junk food, excessive drinking, drugs, etc., are more difficult to understand, at least at first.

I began smoking at the age of fourteen. It was what kids did back then. My parents smoked, as did most of my family members. As I grew up I began to question why I was doing it. I tried repeatedly to stop. I hated the fact that I smoked, and by extension, I was hating myself. I was able to quit several times for a number of years, but it always came back, usually in a moment of weakness! Finally, I decided to stop the war I was waging within. I let go of the judgment of myself for being a smoker. Yes, that's right. I didn't quit smoking, I just quit judging myself for smoking. I decided to use my smoking as a way to learn about myself. I noticed that when I did not smoke there was a low rumbling anger operating beneath the surface. It would often gain power and express as rage. It was scary. I had no option but to take responsibility for my rage and anger. I noticed that right before I would want a cigarette there would be a feeling. The feeling was unpleasant. The cigarette stopped the feeling. Get it? The awareness coupled with the non-judgmental responsibility for my actions, thoughts, and feelings was allowing me to learn about my inner world. It was a novel approach for me at the time.

Peace is the offspring of self-responsibility and conscious awareness. By taking responsibility we are no longer victims in this world. Merging this with a dedication to be aware, we can call a truce on the inner battle and begin to accept ourselves as never before.

I was sitting on a commuter train early one morning, as I did every Monday to Friday. Each day I was tired and uninspired. On this particular day there was a delay and the train sat idle for nearly two hours. Many of the commuters were upset, some slept or read or talked with friends. I sat looking out the window. I saw a weed, growing out of from between the train tracks. It was about a foot tall and had five blue flowers. Effortlessly, the flowers shone their beauty into the world. The gentle breeze moved it from side to side. Watching this plant for a long while I realized that the weed and its flowers were not struggling against their environment, even though it was not ideal. They simply were. No war. No violence. No judgment. They were just there. I saw such beauty in that moment. I felt that beauty touch me deeply. I could be like that weed. I could be me, imperfections and all. I could accept what I could, let go of what was no longer needed, judge nothing, and take full responsibility for all of it. Resistance and struggle, gone. I exhaled deeply, as if releasing a heavy burden. The next inhale was lighter than before. My chest felt freer. I was freer. Peace had landed in my heart.

The experience of feeling peace was humbling. It was the very first time I had ever been aware of feeling peace as an adult. My mind ceased to struggle. My body followed this new instruction and let go of the neck pain I had grown so accustomed to. It was new and exciting. I'm not sure how long the experience lasted, perhaps only a few moments, yet I was irrevocably changed by the experience. I now knew that I could be at peace, regardless of what was happening around me, if I made that choice. Granted, some days are easier than others and some situations more challenging than others.

Can you imagine for a moment? What does peace feel like for you? What does it look like to you? Spending some time in actively imagining peace can be a powerful gateway to a new experience. If you feel called, I invite you to try it out for yourself.

Some people say that it isn't possible to be at peace in a world that is so broken and in conflict. True, there is much that seems broken and there is no denying the conflict. Yet, what if those are reflecting our own inner states of conflict? When I sat on the delayed train I was initially frustrated and annoyed because of the delay and how that was effecting my work day and my ability to meet the expectations of people who were depending on me. Nevertheless, I was still able to feel a moment of peace. It was truly magical. I did not make a choice in that moment on the train. The realization arose within me, perhaps as an act of grace. All I did was let it. No, it didn't make sense in the "normal" way. It didn't need to.

We usually think that something needs to change outside of us, in our experience of what's going on around us, for us to feel good or happy or at peace. This perpetuates a state of victimhood. I certainly have identified with "victim" for much of my life. I can hear the voice of objection arise...I am not a victim! And I ask you to consider if that is really true. Are you in charge of your experience? Do you blame others for your feelings, by saying things like, "She said this horrible thing and made me so mad!?" Do you com-plain about your situation, feeling unfairly treated? Do you justify to yourself and others why you can't do certain things? These types of statements reflect an inner perspective that places our power outside of us and helps to keep us at war with the world and at war within ourselves. It is not so much the feeling like a victim that is the problem, but the intense struggle we feel with being a victim.

Today, in this moment, can you imagine making a declaration for yourself that you will no longer contribute to the energy of war, violence, or blame; even for merely one minute? Can you envision, in your mind's eye, that all those struggles were surrendered into the wind, and effortlessly carried away? Breathe deeply as you visualize. Can you further picture that as you step into this ceasefire there is an open space spontaneously created within you? The burdens are lifted and the struggle within is over. Just for this minute. Can you feel the release? If you don't feel it directly, believe that you can. Your mind slows, your body relaxes, and you feel safe. No war. No violence. No blame, or judgment. Let that space open within you and imagine that you feel a gentle, warm, and loving wave fill the space. Peace.

Each time we take a moment to try this out we are building our Peace Keeper muscles and peace begins to feel more familiar and comfortable.

What happens next is really up to each of us. Learning to embody peace and be its keeper may begin to overflow out into the world, through you. As you experience peace within you there may be a spontaneous, effortless shift that occurs. Anger dissipates and we engage with people is a more peaceful way. Rather than constantly feeling attacked, we may notice that there are times when we are able to not take things others do, or say, personally. If we lead with peace with ourselves and into our connections with others, we will begin to see a change in our relationships.

I have been exploring this way of approaching my life for many years now. I am not perfect at it all day, every day. And that is okay. I am committed to be liberated from that life where I am unaware, victimized, and at war against myself. And when moments of struggle do arise, I aim to approach them from a place of calmness and inquire within to search out what the source of struggle is. As the answer arises within me, I grow and expand into a fuller experience of who I truly am. Stepping boldly and peacefully forward with self-acceptance, self-love, and self-responsibility seems to me a powerful path.

Have you noticed that when we war against something, it never seems to go away? We have, as a society, waged a war on drugs, a war against terror, a war against war, been fighting the battle against cancer, and so many other things that we have deemed to be bad. And I am not saying that any of these things is good or desirable. What I am saying is that as we fight, we continue to feed the very things that we are trying to starve. What if we could suspend our judgments about drugs, sickness, and all the things we don't like? Can you even imagine that it is possible?

This is the point where we are truly transforming how we approach and experience life. Dream it being possible. Imagine it is true. What would our world look like if we all started living from this point of view? Not that we should all do, think, and believe the same things – that would be boring – just that we all lead with peace; the freedom from war and violence in ourselves and in all our relationships. I think this new perspective on peace could be fun to explore!

Let's begin exploring! What is peace? Beyond the simple definition I shared above, I can impart my experience. In the early years of adulthood, I thought peace could only exist if everyone in my life was happy. For some reason I had taken on the role of keeping everyone happy (that's a different story!). I had attached my identity and worth to the level of happiness that the people around me were experiencing. Not surprisingly, I was unhappy a lot and did not feel at peace in any way. Liberating myself from being responsible for the level of happiness that others experienced has been a long and winding journey, and on the way I have had some very amazing things happen. Layer by layer the beliefs that limited my experience of myself were pulled back, and each time I moved into a closer relationship with myself. What I had not anticipated was the sense of peace that began to infiltrate into absolutely all areas of my life.

Emotionally I was experiencing peace as "still waters." Life was happening as it always had, yet I was not reacting to it the same way. Instead of defending myself, I could stand in my confidence. Rather than getting angry, I could see through eyes of empathy and compassion, for myself and others. Quite literally my feelings could show up, be felt, and let go of. I became aware that what I felt was not dictated by anything other than my choice. The still waters felt calm, relaxed, content, and confident.

Physically I began feeling considerably less pain in my body. For years I had struggled with neck, shoulder, and lower back problems that started from a fall when I was fifteen years old. My inner resistance to what was going on in my life was dissolving, and with it went the pain. I began noticing that when I was in pain physically, I was also in pain emotionally. The two went hand-in-hand. When I took responsibility for this awareness and imagined peace within, letting go of resistance and struggle, my body reflected this state. I would sit and allow my body to release stress, fear, and judgment.

Identifying and being responsible for my thoughts was, and remains, my greatest challenge. Like many people, I started out identifying with negative thoughts and thinking the thoughts were me. As I learned to bring more consciousness to bare, and merely acknowledge a thought and not identify as that thought, I started to be able to just observe the thoughts and let them go. As part of the process, I discovered that originally some thoughts had strong meaning attached to them. For example, a thought like "I am fat" can lead to a meaning of "Therefore I am not attractive, or I am lazy." The meaning I gave to a thought was a reflection of the deeper belief systems at work in my mind and were not necessarily true. Making peace with my belief systems allowed them to more readily reveal themselves and consequently opened the way for me to be in a more peaceful state of being.

The result of living as best I can, being willing to take responsibility for my state of being, has been so profound that it brings tears to my eyes.

I woke early one morning. As I lay in bed, I noticed a contentment within me. I had nothing in my mind that demanded to be changed (even though there were still things in my life that weren't optimal). I had no pain in my body (even though I hadn't been exercising or lost any weight) and I felt joy to be just living my life. It was a magical moment.

My conclusion: Peace is possible.

And it is possible for you too!

Susan Kern, M.Sc. has been on a conscious path of self-exploration and healing for over eighteen years. Having healed a chronic illness in herself, she guides people with challenging life and/or health situations to trust that they have what it takes to heal, grow, and expand into their true self. Susan sees the obstacles in life as opportunities for growth and transformation. A scientist, healer, and teacher, Susan nurtures the vision of people living beyond illusion, where they know they are enough, so they can step into loving, accepting, and trusting themselves as the Divine Humans they truly are.

CHAPTER FIFTEEN by Randall Mitchell

Life's Pressure Brings Out Our Perfect Peace

Can one really perfect peace? Is it possible to live a life with no disruption and unexpected crises? Well I'm not here to answer that question. I am here however to share with you a powerful truth, that when fully understood you will have more control over your life!

Peace in a Parable

There's an ancient parable that in its simplicity holds a profound truth. It is in these moments that I'd encourage you to clear your mind, relax your shoulders, and take a deep breath, knowing that what you are about to receive will be exactly what you need for this season in your life. This is your moment to read the tale below as we will zoom in on it thereafter.

> *As evening came, Jesus said to his disciples, "Let's cross to the other side of the lake." So they took Jesus in the boat and started out, leaving the crowds behind (although other boats followed).*
>
> *But soon a fierce storm came up. High waves were breaking into the boat, and it began to fill with water.*
>
> *Jesus was sleeping at the back of the boat with his head on a cushion. The disciples woke him up, shouting, "Teacher, don't you care that we're going to drown?"*
>
> *When Jesus woke up, he rebuked the wind and said to the waves, "Peace! Be Still!"*
>
> *Suddenly the wind stopped, and there was a great calm.*
>
> *Then he asked them, "Why are you afraid? Do you still have no faith?"*
>
> *The disciples were absolutely terrified. "Who is this man?" they asked each other. "Even the wind and waves obey him!"* Mark 4:35-41

If only we had that kind of power. I'm sure we would do much more than calm winds and waves. Coming to think about it, I'm glad that we don't have that kind of power.

As we read in the beginning, they were crossing to the other side of the lake when a fierce storm arose.

Have you ever noticed that whenever you are about to cross over into something new in your life, a fierce storm seems to always appear head-on? Or whenever you want to go to the next level in your life, finances, health, or relationships, there always seems to be something or someone trying to bring you down? Let me start off with saying that this is just the way it's going to be. Just like the disciples, there is no escaping it!

The best part about the parable is in the next statement that Jesus makes: "Peace! Be still!" It's at this moment when the boat was in total chaos and the disciples were absolutely frantic, running to and fro and all they wanted was Peace.

Have you ever found your life in a state of total chaos, running to and fro, desiring nothing but peace? Peace in your body, mind, and soul. I am sure that you've agreed in your spirit to this question however I want to share with you a lesson that I want you to keep with you for the rest of your life. And that is, "Peace, Be Still!"

I believe that in order for Peace to be Perfected, it needs to Pressured. You see, the disciples were desiring peace, however when you look at His response through a different lens, you see that He is actually requesting for Peace to be still.

This is a crucial lesson because we often pray for our problems to be taken away. However, I want you to welcome the chaos, welcome the confusion, welcome the pressure and demand Peace, to be still! Because for our Peace to be Perfected, it needs to Pressured. The more it is pressured, the more accustomed it becomes to that type of pressure. As time progresses, your tolerance matures and the things that use to bother you ten months ago does not bother you anymore.

This is the dichotomy of life. If you desire more peace, you have to know that it's acquired through more pressure. You can't have more of this without more of that!

It is my desire for you to understand that your level of peace is in close coloration with your level of pressure. Take a moment right now and think about that moment in your life where total chaos was the order of the day. All you desired at that moment was a way out. As you reflect back, I am certain that because of that chaotic moment, you are stronger, wiser, and better. Your Peace was perfected just a little because of that moment. Take this thought with you as you go through your journey, knowing that we love you, knowing that we care, and knowing that your Peace is Perfected in the Pressure!

Randall Mitchell has been working his entire life with teens, inspiring them to live out their dreams. He was involved in the South African Radio industry for four years as a Radio Presenter and now hosts a lifestyle/magazine show that airs on Rogers TV. His desire is to see that the development of teen character has a solid foundation and has dedicated his life to helping teens take leadership. Randall has risen above the elements and wants to share ways he has overcome them. You can find those keys in his latest book entitled *"TEENERSHIP – Leadership for Teens"*.

PEACEFUL POINT by Marie Woods

#Peace is Personally Manifested

Peace is...allowing relaxation no matter what circumstances I face.

Peace is...keeping a soft heart.

Peace is...watching the sunrise in the morning.

Peace is...manifesting a long-lost dream.

Peace is...overcoming the obstacles of your past.

Peace is...letting go of mistakes made and keeping the lessons.

Peace is...valuing your time on earth and finding your true purpose.

Peace is...learning a new skill.

Peace is...sharing knowledge.

Peace is...knowing you're beautiful just the way you are.

Peace is...the ability to make another soul shine.

Peace is...passionately loving others.

Peace is...caring when no one else does.

Peace is...extending kindness.

Peace is...pampering yourself.

Peace is...speaking kindly about yourself and others.

Peace is...expressing joy and saying thank you.

Peace is...meditation and praying.

Peace is...lighting a candle.

Peace is...believing in your dreams.

Peace is...spending time in nature and watching the sunset.

Peace is...making a healthy change.

Peace is...loving yourself unconditionally.

Peace is...noticing the love around you.

Peace is...learning to live in the moment.

Peace is...being patient with myself, others, and life itself.

Peace is...being honest with myself and others.

Peace is...knowing that you're a blessing to the world.

Peace is...letting go of what you can't control.

Peace is...staying true to yourself and teaching peace by example.

Peace is...starting my day with powerful affirmations.

Peace is...casting positive words into your future.

Peace is...finding the gift/gem within painful situations.

Peace is...enjoying true intimacy.

Peace is...remembering your magnificence.

Peace is...saying good-bye to guilt and shameful emotions.

Peace is...knowing that you can do anything.

Peace is...giving your worries to God.

Peace is...turning negativity into positive energy.

Peace is...enjoying new friendships and appreciating great friends.

Peace is...knowing you deserve the good in your life.

Peace is...confidently taking chances and dreaming big.

Peace is...opening your heart and using loving words.

Peace is...thanking the universe for unexpected blessings.

Peace is...knowing that you have already won.

Peace is...giving your imagination free reign.

Peace is...acknowledging your inner genius.

Peace is...having a clutter-free environment.

Peace is...appreciating your loved ones.

Peace is...sharing a genuine smile with a stranger.

Peace is...bonding with your children.

Peace is...speaking your mind.

Peace is...traveling to your favorite countries.

Peace is...listening to relaxing music.

Peace is...cooking your favorite dish.

Peace is...trying on your future.

Peace is...enjoying a sense of belonging.

Peace is...knowing that you deserve love and support.

Peace is...savoring the sweetness of life.

Peace is...releasing fear and indecision.

Peace is...enjoying having clear focus and thinking.

Peace is...deciding what kind of day you would like to have.

Peace is...trusting the process.

Peace is...choosing to live blissfully.

Marie Woods, a native of Philadelphia, PA is the colorful, down-to-earth key makeup artist and founder of Fab Face Artistry. Growing up, Marie was filled with profound wonderment and satiated through the world of art. With a longstanding love of art and aesthetics, at just thirty years old, she is skillfully building a platform upon that.

Social Link: www.styleseat.com/mariewoods

CHAPTER SIXTEEN by Troy Smith

Overcoming Human Nature to Find Peace

The nature of peace has many elements. It includes understanding, non-judgment, clarity, acceptance, charity, and joy. Summed up into one word, the nature of peace is love. Every living being has a vision of life perfected. In none of these visions is this perfect life possible without the presence of peace. Anything or situation that brings chaos, hate, or adversarial conditions will never see peace.

If you look at the message of the sages throughout time, all of them have sought one thing – this idea of peace. Though most of them have gone about achieving this goal in misguided ways, the object has always been the same: to create a life full of joy that is devoid of disturbance.

One of the major hurdles to attaining this ultimate state has been the lack mentality. The lack mentality is one that believes there is only a limited amount of resources in this world. The only way to have peace and joy is to take from someone else what they currently enjoy. This mentality, by its very nature, is the opposite of peace.

Peace is attained from first understanding that there is no lack. For every person, being, nation, and planet, there is always enough. The secret is to share, not hoard or covet anything. It comes from standing in a place that seeks to see a perspective through the eyes of another, remembering that we all come from the same source and essentially have the same desires. It reveals itself through clarity. The more we take a look and at least attempt to feel the heart of another, peace can then begin to shine in our lives. Who amongst us does not wish the best for our families and loved ones? Who amongst us believes that these so called others do not wish the same? Becoming clear on this universal desire can usher in a state of tranquility.

Peace comes from acceptance. It breaches all boundaries when we learn to embrace the perceived differences between us all. When we learn to see things as valid from others perspectives, we allow peace to reign. All are great, none is truly above another. If we can learn to accept and embrace this fact, peace is given its opportunity to reign supreme.

Peace comes from charity. When we see another in need, we are given the opportunity to be blessed with peace. This opportunity comes because we are able to demonstrate to another that there is always enough. We are able to feel the satisfaction that comes from giving. This feeling is not boastful, it is thankful. It comes to strengthen the bond between us all. What we see as charity to another is truly a blessing to ourselves.

Peace comes from joy. When the heart is pleased, and the spirit is wrapped in the realization of oneness, peace is achieved. Joy is when the soul dances. While dancing alone can be satisfactory, having a partner allows it to grow exponentially. The joyous feeling is the perfect environment for creativity to flow. It makes for fertile ground and glorious, nourishing sunshine. It is the place where all life thrives!

In summary, all of these elements are pieces of love. Blended together they bring a result of peace. Focused on and allowed to thrive, they bring peace perfected.

> *"And the fruit of righteousness is sown in peace of them that make peace."* James 3:18 KJV

This verse tells us that beautiful things and experiences come to those who bring peace. Here we are told that man is the bringer of peace. It suggests that peace is a choice, an experience that we can and should bring to our lives. With this effort, this desire, this intention will come the fruit of righteousness which I interpret to be the joys of life.

> *"Peace does not mean an absence of conflicts; differences will always be there. Peace means solving these differences through peaceful means; through dialogue, education, knowledge; and through humane ways."*
> Dalai Lama XIV

In the above quote, the Dalai Lama expresses that peace does not mean there is an absence of conflict. It recognizes that there will be opposing views. Peace embraces this and seeks to find common ground through constructive communication, education, and means that will foster growth and understanding. This wise and peaceful being has witnessed enough hate to drive most of us insane. He however is known as one of the most peaceful beings in existence. Where does he get this wondrous state of peace from? He gets it from his soul, his heart. He understands that it is the falsely perceived separation of man, the sense of desperation, the feeling of lack that must be addressed. He understands that peace comes from inclusion, and not exclusion. He understands that peace comes from love! All of the conflicts in this world could peaceably be solved if all men would accept this truth.

I would now like to share with you a story I've never told before told. I trust you will be able to see the significance for our society today.

A man marries a woman who has three daughters. He also has a young girl of his own and the couple proceed to have a daughter together. That makes five lovely girls for this couple. The joy and love flowed freely through the home of this newly formed family. Less than a month after the youngest blessing is born, the eldest of their beautiful children unexpectedly dies due to unforeseen circumstances.

The family is devastated by their loss and prays that justice is served and there is a resolution to their distressing ordeal. Unfortunately, things did not turn out the way they had hoped it would. The father goes through each day confused and angry. At this point, he thinks to himself, "Will justice ever be served?" Suddenly, something comes over him. It is in this moment, an overwhelming feeling of love washes through him. In this moment alone, forgiveness and love uses its awesome power to heal! Love gives peace to this man when he needs it the most.

Now, let's break down some of the elements of this story. The man and his new family were in a pure state of joy. They had welcomed a new daughter to their family and had big hopes for their future. A disturbing loss turned their lives upside down. In a single moment, their lives turned from joy to chaos.

They had hoped that at least justice would be served for their loved one. Thankfully, his heart was still open to hearing the true desires of his spirit. In this pivotal moment, love swoops in and reigns supreme. In that moment, he understood that, *"Hate can never drive out hate; only love can do that."* Martin Luther King, Jr. If he were to "take his revenge", more of the chaos that turned his life upside down would ensue. The peace he so desperately sought would certainly not be allowed to shine through.

How do we find this thing called peace? We find it by silencing our mind. We find it by listening to the quiet voice in our heart that connects all of us.

So what are we learning from these lessons of Peace? We have learned that Peace comes from Love. It is found inside the hearts of men as given from their spirit. It brings balance and beauty anytime it is allowed to express itself. It is a choice that is offered and accepted. Peace be unto you all!

Troy Smith is a Coach, Consultant, Speaker, and Trainer whose focus is to help others discover the power within themselves. As a life-long student of spirituality, he has infused his style of empowerment with what he considers to be the ultimate truth. Professionally, Troy has spent the last thirty-plus years in corporate and private industry management. During those years, he has been consistently tasked with building effective and productive teams. To facilitate that, he has studied coaching, psychology, spirituality, and systems extensively. He considers the ultimate truth to be love and uses that belief to help create a world that we all can thrive in.

PEACEFUL POINT by Diana Alli D'souza

#Peace is You and Me

Peace is a beautiful thing; it starts with you and me. We can move mountains together in solidarity. We can break cycles of conflict and bring peace to the people in this world. We don't need to be slaves of blame and hatred. We can be nurturers of world peace, starting with you and me unifying our hearts first; we then have the strength to transform the world.

I can vividly remember the dreadful 2001 tragedy in the USA with all the devastation affecting thousands of lives. Families and friends lost their loved ones; a community and world left distraught. I was at a medical school then, a senior staff member and counselor overseeing student life, witnessing this catastrophe unfold live on television. Students were afraid for their lives citing copycats destroying places of worship. In the wake of this international tragedy, it was emotional to witness students, faculty, multi-faith leaders and the public-at-large come together in prayer and solidarity. I attended several of these daily prayer forums at medical school, across the University and in faith centres. Our Canadian friends were willing to let go of differences and embrace each other in interfaith dialogue. What was unique is our prayers had a common universal theme: loving our one God.

Most of us are capable of being united with warm open hearts. We as a force are capable of contributing to peace and harmony, mindfully and with purpose – one person, one step, one moment, one day at a time. If only we focus on our gentleness, kindness, peacefulness, joyfulness, and hopefulness – using the core values of understanding, patience, compassion, forgiveness, and respect – in ourselves, our families, our community, and our planet, we can become the change agents of peace in our world. We need to look beyond ourselves through a global lens, making our difference in small ways. Eventually it will lead to the greater good of society. What better way to start by making our world a better place to live in. Let there be peace on earth, and let it begin with you and me.

A perfect quote says it all:

> You can expand to infinity – it all depends on your courage. And courage also comes as your experience grows, as you see the more you expand, the more beautiful life becomes; the more you expand, the more love showers on you; the more you expand, everything take on a new psychedelic dimension. It becomes more colorful, more alive, more dancing. The

ordinary world suddenly starts changing into something extraordinary. The mundane becomes the sacred and these are the most significant moments in life – when the mundane become sacred. Osho

Diana Alli D'souza has founded/co-founded and facilitated nationally recognized outreach programs in the Faculty of Medicine, University of Toronto. Diana has served on numerous Boards: Governing Council, community foundations, local/national committees. She is the recipient of numerous awards, the prestigious Order of Ontario and the Queen Elizabeth II Diamond Jubilee Medal, and community recognition.

http://accessempowermentcouncil.org/our-team.html

CHAPTER SEVENTEEN by Mary Hilty

Finding the Pathway to My Peace

I remember so many times from my past where I truly sensed as if I would never feel quiet and balanced. I struggled with the fast-paced life we all are a part of. I worried what people said and what they were doing. I actually consciously watched others and thought deeply about what their lives must be like. At times I experienced some envy about where they were and where I was in life. Thankfully, none of it means a thing to me anymore. People are just amazing! When I watch now, what they are doing in their lives interests me deeply. I feel so humbled and happy to be able to witness it all without judgment or envy. I have learned that it's just fine for me to be me and it's just fine for others to be who and what they are. All of the "feel good" commentary from my parents was not mumble-jumble. They actually were handing over the great gift of simplicity.

We moved numerous times as kids and much later (after I had moved out on my own) I discovered that we relocated all of the time because my family tried to stay ahead of bill collectors. The true beauty of it all is that I had this amazing childhood with truly loving people all around me and I never knew any down side. When this information was passed to me, I made up my mind very quickly not to feel shame, embarrassment, anger...none of that, because I now had new information. I knew deep in my heart that it was still the same wonderfully interesting childhood. I made a distinct choice not to go back and review that which I never had any control over. Like so many things which come up in a life – anybody's life – our first order of business is to decide what we do with the information. If it is about something that already happened, then clearly the ability to change it is not a part of what we have to think about. Our next decision will only have to do with how we handle the truth. What happened in the past is the truth...like it or nay, and our only avenue of action is to decide how it works or does not work in our lives. We can be affected by those things behind us, but we cannot change them. They are cemented in history.

I make the choice not to be consumed by the actions of others, not to be resentful, hateful or spiteful, and to always find some-thing wonderful from which to make forward movement. All of our opinions are truly just our own perceptions of how things make us "feel." Generally, it is in our own best interests to chill-out and not voice them. It is extremely important for us to pay attention to everything going on around us, but accepting the fact that we shouldn't feel the need to be a player in every scenario. We understand so much when we hang back and silently learn from others. Most of our significant learning comes from our inner voice holding us in check while we "react" instead of "responding" to outside stimuli. You and I know the little triggers that somehow turn us into monsters with our fellow humans when we stick our faces where they do not need to be. Because, by golly, we just must have our opinion heard. The truth: We do not need to have it heard.

The quest for a peaceful life is so much fun. The first step we have to take is to get rid of judgment. There is no way we can feel peace if we are internally judging and resenting everything we see, hear, read, or overhear. That requires a large amount of space in our heads, and then we have little or no space left for appreciation and gratitude. There is no pathway to peace without appreciation and gratitude. It is vitally important to learn how to see, hear, read and overhear without getting all tied up in knots over it. Everything we take in will be replaced by more of the same in an hour, a day, a week, a month, a year...and finally a whole lifetime. This is our own lifespan and the choices we make truly carve out the nature of our lives. All of the choices begin with communication. We can monitor and control that within our experiences.

Our Peace is dependent upon our own behavior. We have to make promises to our own selves and we must learn to keep those commitments. If every promise made to self is not broadcast – but worked through – eventually we deepen our own relationship with ourselves and, believe it or not, by not breaking our promises to self, we learn how to trust ourselves. That is the beginning of our own personal doorway to peace – trusting ourselves. Only when we honestly and fully have confidence in ourselves do we deepen our trust with others.

I am not looking for everything that is wrong in the world, I'm looking for everything that is right. The wrong stuff is hyped up on the news, sensationalized, propagandized, and becomes highly visible gossip. We cluck our tongues at the horrors of the news while watching all the way to the end of the broadcasts and we become fearful, jaded, opinionated, and ultimately crippled with our lack of being able to solve anything. The reason it is such an impossible situation is that we are not working together to find solutions. We are watching a box in our homes. So much is thrown at us in a single broadcast that it becomes really difficult to wade through it all. I can find something wrong with everything, everyone, every situation, every item...if I only give it an ounce of effort. I can also find something right...if I only give it the same amount of effort. Choose to find the good stuff. And once you find that, shout it from the rooftops! Share it with your neighbors.

I know what I feel in my heart when I am morose, saddened, depressed, filled with judgment, full of arrogance, and loathing. I feel utterly alone, as in lonely...not alone as in being in my own company. When we allow ourselves to hunker down into a dark emotional abyss, we do not have the strength to haul ourselves up and out of the mess. It is easier to learn not to go to those places than it is to get back from them. When I feel one of these weird places opening wide for me to enter, I get out of there. I grab my keys, take a drive, talk to people, or take a walk. But no matter what I do to ward off the "uglies", it will always involve talking with people.

When I was a little girl, and I am talking little here, my Mom would say upon my waking in the morning, "Before you put those little toes on the floor, it's important to spend some time deciding what kind of day you want. Do you want a good day? Do you want a bad day? Choose and then get out of bed." I learned from that parental guidance and I still practice the exercise today. Believe me, when we are participating consciously with our choices, they become easier and less conscious as we move through our lives on the road to our own Peace. If we make some basic and profoundly simple rules for ourselves, we can get to a peaceful place and stay there.

I was also told by my highly motivating Mother to, "Quit with the moaning and groaning about everything you have to get done and just do it! If you act like this is the first time and the last time you will ever be able to do it (whatever it is), I promise you will have a different attitude and a better outcome." Of course that bit of wisdom has been incorporated into my personal quest to live in a peaceful and purposeful place. Funny...all that wisdom thrown at me as a child continues to resonate in my adult thinking.

I do not gossip. It is an amazingly colossal waste of time and energy. Every single time we say something ugly or nasty about others, the Universe is going to give us a lesson on whatever we said. People are all up on Karma today and most do not realize that their own behaviors create their own Karma as they go. It does. Do not bear false witness upon thy neighbor. Shutta you mouth...and when speaking of others, bring their finest attributes, and only those, into the conversation. Do you know what an example is being set in the hearts of others when you do this? If done often enough, soon your entire circle of influence will ac-quire this amazing characteristic. It really does work.

I find peace everywhere I leave peace. I know that seems conceptually hard to understand. Yet it truly is easy. Go to a place of love within yourself and every single time some crummy, horrible thing enters into your mind, slap it away and replace it with a loving thought and a loving prayer to go along. The road to our own peace begins and ends with our ability to teach ourselves to love without conditions and judgment. The truth is living right inside of our own behaviors – right smack dab in our faces. Live a little, love a lot. Think. Be happy with everything and be grateful for it all. If there could be a single formula worldwide for peace, I am certain it would be built on a solid foundation of gratitude. It is not just a word, it is not just an action, it is not something that lives outside of us. It lives within and is the driving force of our lives. When we are grateful and feel thankful, we are better people...more peaceful people.

Peace is not illusive. Peace is not something others have that we cannot also possess. Peace is for all of us. It is our hearts, our souls, our love, and our ability to love. It is gratitude when we take and charity when we give. It is the "higher ground" everyone seeks. It all begins with believing that we can have it. Because we can!

Mary Hilty has written extensively through journaling, composing poems, and a variety of articles. She considers her social interactions with people to be one of her greatest inspiration for writing, which she has been doing most of her life. Mary values her collection of wonderful books, and enjoys gardening, preserving all kinds of foods, and leading a natural lifestyle. She is a mother, grandmother, wife, sister, and friend. A favorite dream is to co-create with other authors and leave her "best self" in the world through writing!

PEACE IS PERFECTED

CHAPTER EIGHTEEN by Anita Sechesky

Peace is Perfected

What are the many ways that you have witnessed or experienced the most beautiful or perfect feeling of peace and tranquility? Did it take having to step away from the busy commotions of life to rediscover the beauty in the world around you? Or did you create a peaceful oasis in your own home and natural surroundings, with little things like candles, incense, or moments of relaxation?

My reason for including this as the third theme within this beautiful anthology is that I've come to understand that peace is something we are always going to look to perfect whether we realize it or not. Once you have had a taste of something that envelops your very soul to that of total bliss and happiness, why wouldn't you choose to have more? We are all connected and with that conscious awareness, we can come to a greater appreciation of attaining this added value to our lives. We constantly long for this fulfilling desire to quench our souls into the luxury and necessity of personal and peaceful perfection.

Although luxurious self-care is something that's not freely allotted to everyone, we can still achieve simple and healing opportunities as we go about our daily lives in a world that is constantly changing. Social media has made it seem that the world is in our backyard, therefore when others are affected by events or circumstances, we begin to feel this overwhelming burden also. We are prompted to conjure emotional responses based on the fact that we are empathetic beings with a greater outreach through our connections, so we always share life experiences and memories with others regardless of the situation. This is when a person begins to understand how valuable their small acts of peace and kindness are towards others, as it creates a perfect balance in our own environment and ultimately becomes a heart-warming experience for everyone else we are associated with.

I believe that in order for peace to be perfected in our lives, one must truly learn to love themselves and those close to them in order to appreciate anyone outside their immediate circle without hesitancy. Otherwise, how could anyone honestly live at peace with those whom they have no natural connection? The true power in loving yourself opens up the reality that we are choosing to accept all of our imperfections. As we willingly choose to think this way, it becomes easier to accept everyone as well, imperfections and all. Keep in mind, this also requires you to let go of everything that does not serve your greatest self any longer. Choosing to love your inner circle connections or those who know and appreciate you sets your loving peace apart for that of our outside world. If you don't allow others to negatively influence you any longer, you'll always create peace around you everywhere you go. Once you have made your peaceful intentions clear and focused, peace will always find its way back to you. You are a peaceful person and deserve to live a life filled with unlimited peace and abundance. This mindset increases the vibrations around you, and positively affects the way that you see yourself, and how others will see you as well.

When you reflect the amount of wasted time and energy it takes to create drama and stress in our lives, do you really want to engage in anything that takes you from manifesting a life of wholeness and well-being? There are so many people walking around us already filled with turmoil and pain. The stressful baggage they choose to carry every day, is not getting any lighter as it just keeps attracting more and more negativity and harm. I believe it takes a person with a big heart to be grateful for the life they have, all the relationships they've been blessed with. Choosing to live in gratitude towards others will always build a better life.

This world is filled with people who possess so much peaceful potential, yet they still feel hopeless and distraught. They no longer have dreams or desires because they are discouraged and demoralized by the traumatic or painful events they keep reliving in their daily lives. This is a testament to why I believe there is so much more remaining for everyone to do when it comes to perfecting the peace in, and around us. If we choose to help others who are hopeless and without peace, find healing for themselves and their loved ones, then we have brought a little piece of heaven to earth.

Our world is filled with so many beautiful and yet broken people. Thankfully, I've had the privilege to provided nursing care to people from various regions around the world, opening my own eyes to what is happening to others in my own neighborhood. My experiences always left me feeling concerned, they are just like everyone else, people need to be loved and accepted to heal. People need a peaceful environment to thrive and live fulfilled lives, regardless of where they are on this planet. I choose to see value in everyone equally. What an amazing world full of precious souls we have yet to reach, one life, one voice, one song that is perfected by the resounding beauty of peace that is felt throughout all the ages, nations, and races. Let's help create peace in every corner of the globe and apply liberally with love, empathy, and grace. We can all do our part to instill peace in each heart we meet on our journey in life. Peace is perfected through one life, one interaction at a time

Anita Sechesky is a Best-Seller Publisher, Registered Nurse, Certified Professional Coach, NLP and LOA Wealth Practitioner, Best-Seller Consultant, multiple International Best-Selling Author, as well as a Workshop Facilitator and Conference Host. She is the Founder and CEO of Anita Sechesky - Living Without Limitations Inc. and the Founder and Publisher of LWL PUBLISHING HOUSE. Anita was born in Guyana, South America and moved to Canada when she was only four years old. Assisting many people to break through their own limiting beliefs in life and business, Anita had discovered her passion to help individuals release their stories in-to successful publications. She has five Best-Selling books, including four anthologies, in which approximately 200 authors and co-authors have benefited to date from her expertise. Anita launched her first solo book *"Absolutely You – Overcome False Limitations and Reach Your Full Potential"* in November 2014. As a Best-Seller Publisher, Anita helps people to put their positive perspectives into print.

CHAPTER NINETEEN by Tim Rahija

Creating the Ultimate Life of Peace

I remember a great quote about peace some years ago and can't recall if it was from a movie or something I read, but it has always stuck with me. The first part was "Peace is not just the absence of conflict..." In considering the message I want to convey, and get to the heart of the matter to really provide meaning and inspiration, I did some research into the basic quote and I found some awesome examples I would like to share.

There is no way to peace, peace is the way - A.J. Muste

Each one has to find his peace from within. And peace to be real must be unaffected by outside circumstances - Gandhi

Peace comes from within, do not seek it without – Buddha

Peace is not something you wish for; It's something you make, something you do, something you are, and something you give away" - Robert Fulghum

Peace is not merely a distant goal that we seek, but a means by which we arrive at that goal - Martin Luther King, Jr.

Just in my own reading of these quotes and allowing them to marinate in my spirit, I discovered a greater appreciation for my own philosophy and greater insights into the general philosophy that has existed for thousands of years.

Peace, like happiness, is the emotion and vibrational state we create from within, and extends to our entire being; to all 50–70 trillion cells that comprise the body. The key is in taking into account that everything in the universe at the quantum level is energy and vibration, and we are all a part of that single ocean of energy. That is our intimate connection to the divine and to all of creation since the beginning of time, through all the ages, and gives us the divine capability to change the world around us by changing what happens inside us. The peace that we choose to create, feel, and believe is one of the essential elements that allows us to shape our reality and thus what happens around us in the world.

I would like to provide an example of how emotional energy is immediately transferred and can change the vibrational state of things and people around us. Consider a room full of people who are positive, happy, and having a good time together. Would think that room has a high level of positive energy? You bet it does. Now, bring in someone who may be feeling hurt, depressed, and down on themselves. Odds are they are not going to be feeling very happy and at peace. However, when they enter the room they are going to feel the positive energy from others and it will help raise their own vibrational state to where they are likely to forget about being down and depressed, they'll be able to smile and laugh, their posture will change, and they may even realize they had the ability to change their emotions and energy level any time they wanted to. In other words, they are now beginning to resonate with the energy level of others in the room. Now you can reverse the scenario and have a room full of people who are angry, bitter, and not in a very good mood and in walks someone who is positive, happy, and cheerful. That person will immediately feel the negative energy and it will impact their own vibrational state, both mentally and physically, that they will do one of two things. They will either start to feel the negativity and become negative as well, or they will choose to leave because they feel repulsed by the negative energy. By these examples, you can see how the change in vibrational energy affects the mental and physical. That is why I stress the importance of choosing the vibrational state you want to be at in order to create and experience greater happiness and a more perfect peace.

By virtue of our emotions, what we feel, how we think, how we act, in terms of peace that we wish to create and experience, we create a certain "template" that is an integral part of our consciousness. And, in the greater, infinite field of consciousness that is the universe, it would appear there is no clear defined boundary that tells us just where we stop and the rest of the universe begins, because the universe is holographic in nature and we each are a part of the larger whole of consciousness. What we create inside in terms of a template of peace is what we give the universe to work with and is what's returned to us as our reality. Peace is not an abstract concept. It is embodied in values, beliefs, our attitude, how we view ourselves, how we view the world, how we treat others, and how we choose to live our lives.

Just imagine for a moment the degree of true peace you can experience in your own life by simply making changes in your thoughts, feelings, emotions, and beliefs. Each of these elements begins and ends with you and no one else. You are the creator and master architect of your personal peace. Each of these elements is a divine act of creation because they emanate from within.

One mistake we often make is the false belief that emotions and our inner peace are caused or affected by external events. In this modern, consumption-driven society we are constantly be bombarded with advertisements and messages that falsely condition many to believe they need the latest, greatest gadget, phone, car, or whatever to experience happiness and peace. We are conditioned to believe "I'll be happy and have peace when..." Peace comes from within, not from without. You could be completely insulated from the external world with absolutely no knowledge of what is happening, yet what you experience internally in that time is the sole product of your own thoughts, feelings, and emotions. You alone are responsible for you.

The external world has no influence on what you experience inside other than that which you allow. There is little doubt that the world is still a dangerous place, full of conflict and chaos, and with today's 24/7 news cycle, you'd be led to believe conflict and chaos is all that is happening in the world. That is just sensationalism and is not a true reflection or representation of the state of humanity because chaos and conflict are not a natural part of the human condition. Why then would anyone want that in their life and diminish the peace that is their birthright? What we choose to focus on is what we create.

Intellect and wisdom give us a much deeper connection between mind and spirit, and thus allows us to experience greater peace in our lives. The key is in understanding the nature of your thoughts in that they are fluid, and you are not your thoughts. You are something much bigger. You are the one perceiving your thoughts, taking notice of life happening around you and what is happening inside you, and you can shape it and mold it at will to better serve you. Remember that internal peace, like happiness, is subjective because it is relative to the individual. What works for one person may not necessarily work for another. You as an individual are as unique a part of God's miraculous creation as are your thoughts, feelings, and emotions. They are unique because you created them and gave them life.

When you do not attach yourself to your thoughts as if they are true, you erase the mental illusions you have created, and your mind and spirit return to their natural, peaceful state. There are times when we experience peace and clarity and sometimes we don't, just as sometimes we experience the sun and clear blue skies and sometimes we don't. We know the sun is always there behind the clouds. Mental peace, clarity, and wisdom are always there, behind our thoughts. Just as the clouds will always part to reveal clear, sunny skies, thoughts roll in and thoughts roll out. You access the peace and clarity that lies beneath your thoughts, and that is where you find yourself. Peace and clarity are only a thought and belief away. But how do you access the clarity and wisdom that underlies thought? How do you return to a more natural state of peace? Some people meditate, some exercise or go for a walk, some play music or practice an art, or simply take a nap. It is up to you to discover what works best for you. The key is in being present in the moment and letting your spirit flow naturally.

Peace is not a tangible object to be chased after. Peace is who you are and your relationship with self and the universe.

Remember, it's your choice to create the ultimate peace you wish to experience in life.

Tim Rahija is a Spiritual Entrepreneur and an International Best-Selling author, having contributed to *"Living Without Limitations – 30 Stories to Heal Your World"* and *"#LOVE – A New Generation of Hope."* He has prior professional experience in Law Enforcement, US Army, Human Resource Management, Information Technology, and Aviation Maintenance. Tim is the founder of his own mobile application development company, with additional business ventures in other technology platforms, life coaching, and personal development. Tim has earned degrees in Human Resource Management from Mid America Nazarene College in 1989, and graduated summa cum laude from DeVry University with a B.Sc. in Information Technology in 2004.

https://www.facebook.com/Tim-Rahija-Bridging-Science-and-Spirituality-913147795403434

timothy.rahija@gmail.com

PEACEFUL POINT by Darla Ouellette

#Peace Within Prayer

She closes her eyes, takes a deep breath, and listens to the birds chirping around her. She enjoys the warm glistening sun radiating on her skin. She tries her best to clear her mind, but has been so stressed out lately. She wants to let it all go, but her mind still races. She takes another deep breath and tries to drown out the noises around her. Dogs are barking in the near distance and the smell of barbecue and home cooking fill the air. Loud music blares from a neighbor's house as they laugh and enjoy themselves on this hot summer day.

She tries to focus once more and is able to let herself relax a little. She feels the tension slowly begin to fade from her neck and shoulders. She adjusts herself in her chair and breathes a little deeper, but is not quite able to clear her mind...what about the laundry, dishes, and vacuuming? She shakes her head and brings herself back to focusing on letting it all go. She centers herself, breathes again, and begins this time to pray. She prays for help learning to relax – to let go of all the tensions in her body. She prays the stress will be released from her body and mind, for help and guidance in her life, and the reassurance that she will get through all the difficult times she has been facing. She feels a slight breeze through the air now. She has been trying to meditate and find her inner peace for a while now, and is determined to find peace and calmness in her life. She asks God for her struggles to end and for peace to take its place within her heart. She thanks Him for all she has, and lets the gratitude and serenity wash over her. She is grateful that He is always there for her and helping her through every tough situation. She stretches her arms out as if to give God a Hug and she feels His loving embrace in return.

She sinks back in her chair, opens her eyes, and smiles. Even with her often stressful life and difficult times she has faced, she always has God. He has always been there for her, and her faith in Him has pulled her through. This is how she fills herself back up with inner peace.

Darla Ouellette is an accomplished Registered Nurse. She also holds diplomas for her RPN and Law and Security Administration. Darla is a devoted mother to her wonderful son Cameron, is certified as a Law Of Attraction Life Coach, and has always had a passion for writing.

https://ca.linkedin.com/pub/darla-ouellette

CHAPTER TWENTY by Candace Hawkshaw

Life Seasons of Peace

Going with the flow of the seasons in nature has brought such peace within me. Each season presents its own special aspect of peace to me: spring – new beginnings, summer – creativity, fall – harvesting and letting go, winter – hibernation and going deep within.

I am a teacher of Reiki. Learning and teaching Reiki has helped me become more connected with my inner peace, combining the healing energy of Mother Earth with Reiki to heal myself and others. As a teacher of Reiki, I feel it is critical for my students to be connected with Mother Earth - when we heal, so does she.

I am blessed that the farm I grew up on remains in the family. It still teaches me the wonders and magic of each season.

My life of responsibility started young. I was married at eighteen, had my first child at nineteen and twins at twenty-three. At that time, I followed the norm of society and never really thought about peace. However, on turning fifty, I feel I started my second life. It has taken me years to actually feel, understand, and know the peace that I had felt as a child; running outside, dancing like no one was watching, and only returning home when I heard my mom's special call. Peace was outside in Nature – my soul and spirit soaring...just being...not a care in the world. No matter what the season, I always went outside. Now, as I play with my grandchildren, I find myself not worrying about what others think. It has brought memories of the freedom I had as a child. Being with them in the moment and one with them, and allowing my inner child to come out brings me joy and peace. There is such unconditional love. I share the seasons with them, showing them the magic in the natural world, and how to co-create, appreciate, and learn.

Mother Nature is a one of our greatest teachers of growth, regrowth, and new beginnings. No matter what chaos or negativity happens, she always shows me beauty, love, and healing. For me, one of the healthiest ways to stay at peace, be balanced, grounded, and centered in the midst of the fear, sadness, and chaos in the world, is to take some breaks several times a day and tap into the healing of Mother Nature. She handles change much more gracefully than most of humanity does; I have learned this from her.

I have grown to know that the four seasons each has magic and gifts for me if I stop, look, and listen, and become aware of my surroundings and my environment – her nature spirits, her sounds, her beauty. When I am one with her I respect her and her nature spirits as they are meant to be here, just as I am.

Spring is the season of awakening, fresh ideas, new beginnings, and life begins to emerge. I am in awe of how the flowers start to peek out of the ground and the green of the grass starts to show. Even if an unexpected snowfall happens, these beautiful spirits still emerge. I have walked through the forest and have seen how a tree or plant is growing in what would seem to be hardest place to grow. Nature does not stop when there are kinks in their way. I see babies being born, be it a bird or deer. Sap is flowing; time to collect what the maple trees have created to become beautiful syrup filled with so many wonderful health benefits and spiritual satisfaction. Once Mother Earth has warmed up and is ready, I plant my seeds of vegetables and herbs. When I do, I hold them in my hands and thank them and the soil. I call in Reiki and bless them with love and gratitude. I start going barefoot and feel the earth beneath my feet. I sing and dance with gratitude for the blessings these seeds and season will bring.

Summer is the season of creativity. I feel the heat of the sun and see the grass getting greener, and the flowers and trees in full bloom. Weeding my garden, being in silence, being one with nature, barefoot and bare handed brings peace to my soul and spirit. I watch the hawks soaring. I go to the lake, play in the water, or just sit outside and enjoy the warmth and the breeze. I go on adventures camping or hiking. I watch sunsets, sunrises, and the stars and the moon whilst sitting at an open fire. I walk in the warm rain and feel it washing away sadness or negativity. I dance in the rain like no one is watching, and jump in puddles.

Fall is the season of harvesting and letting go. I, like the trees releasing their leaves of radiant colors of red, gold, and orange, look at what no longer serves me; I take it off and let it go. It is time to harvest the seeds I planted in the spring, now grown. It is time to harvest them – drying, freezing, canning, or preserving. There is nothing like picking a bean off the vine and just eating it right there. Or a carrot, freshly pulled from the ground, the dirt wiped off and then eaten. The taste is astounding. I have such gratitude seeing all my vegetables together in a bowl – greens, oranges, reds, yellows. I emulate the smaller animal spirits who also collect and gather food for the winter.

Winter is the season of hibernation and accessing my deepest wisdom. The trees go to sleep; some animals hibernate or fly south. I love to walk in the wintry forest and hear the crunching of the snow. Snowshoeing is a relaxing activity and can take me into places I could normally not walk. Having snow on the ground allows me to see foot prints of any animals that have gone ahead of me. Mother Nature brings us once again a beautiful white blanket of snow to cleanse and purify the Earth. Solstice is a special time of year I cherish with family and friends, bringing in traditions of baking to acknowledge our ancestors.

We are not separate from Mother Nature; we are one – the air we breathe, the water in our body. When I connect with Nature, there is no judgment, no telling me what to do, no telling me who I am. I show up in Nature authentically. She can guide me if I am aware. Animals give me affirmations and peace within. She communicates to me through all my physical senses. There is sweetness in the air, and the smell of rain. A robin appears after a long winter. A hawk soars. A blue jay sings. A crow caws. A fox comes out of the forest and looks at me. A deer walks in front of me and takes my breath away. A rainbow appears after a warm rain. The rustling sounds of the trees blowing in the wind. The exploding flavor of strawberries and raspberries. The sweet taste of the sap dripping from the maple tree. Thistles pricking my fingertip. The warmth of the earth beneath my feet. All these stir and touch my senses with a message.

For me to be in balance, to be at peace, and to keep my intuition open, I connect and ground myself with Mother Earth, call in Reiki, and go with the flow of her seasons.

Candace Hawkshaw is a certified Holy Fire II Reiki Master Teacher and a Spiritual Teacher. She is a Certified Soul Realignment Practitioner, a certified Reflexologist, a certified Acupressure Practitioner, and a certified Black Pearl Practitioner. She is an entrepreneur and her business is called Soaring Spirit. Candace has written her story in two books: *"Ruby Red Shoes – Empowering Stories on Relationships, intuition & Purpose"* and *"Living Without Limitations – Vision Quest."* She is compiling her own anthology book titled *"Love is The Most Powerful Energy in The Universe – Stories of Love's Healing Journeys"* which is due to be released in 2016.

CHAPTER TWENTY-ONE by Janine Moore

Get in Touch with Your Soul to save Our Planet

What if climate change and our current economic unrest are setting the stage to transform our world in a more positive way? This may be a wake-up call to grow our humanity and create a better, more peaceful world.

We're awakening to the fact that in wounding the earth, we've harmed ourselves. Global pollution and our inner pollution are related. Collectively, we've wounded our planet and together we can heal her. Our outer world reflects our inner world. Our busy, cluttered, over-stimulated lives create stress and exhaustion. We need a different path.

It's important to begin with a vision of the world you want to live in and then align your thoughts and actions to get there. Anything toxic will need to be removed. It's essential to get in touch with what really matters. Begin by reconnecting with nature.

We yearn for the peaceful mystery and wonder that nature provides. Yet, we're often out of touch with our natural world. Nature can soothe our soul, yet it's often ignored.

We take a three week guided tour and expect nature to show up on our schedule. "What time do the whales swim by?" I've been asked on the West Coast. Visitors left disappointed when I explained they have their own time frame.

Waiting for my Island ferry, I saw an eagle catch a gull and eat if for lunch, while a boy on a bench studied his cell phone. Spontaneous acts of nature were not on his agenda that day.

We're distracted. We're connected with technology most of the day and night but not with the world around us. Now's the time to connect with what it is our soul is asking for so we can create our own peace and joy.

Simplify your life. Surround yourself with natural beauty.

Choose Your Lifestyle First

Spend most of your time doing things you enjoy. Look within to identify what you really care about. Get in touch with your soul. Acknowledge what will serve your life best. Choose to live in conscious alignment with your core values.

We're starting to let go of our materialistic consumer culture that focuses heavily on the quantity of possessions we can accumulate. We're moving towards a higher quality of life reflected in better physical, emotional, and spiritual well-being. We're shedding stuff so we can have more time for experiences.

Meaningful Work

We're disillusioned with the nine to five job grind and want more freedom and flexibility. We're tired of being cogs in the wheel of a large bureaucracy.

We're searching for meaningful work that serves a purpose. We want to express our inborn gifts and authentic self in our work.

Community

Collaboration is on the rise. We want shared experiences. We're sharing cars, spare rooms, and workspaces. Together, we're creating green products, growing local food, and developing alternative energy. Working in a supportive community improves mental health and creates harmony.

Our new economy will emerge out of brainstorming ideas and co-creating with other entrepreneurs.

We're beginning to resonate with the wisdom and peace of First Nation cultures. Western civilization has suffered because we've disregarded these values for too long.

Traditional First Nation cultures teach the importance of shared values in alignment with nature. They view these as the four basic components of self-esteem:

1] **Belonging:** Treat all others as your relatives. This includes not only people, but also animals and plants. All need to live in harmony, with a sense of shared community based on love.

2] **Mastery:** Each person is encouraged to develop self-mastery and self-actualization based on inborn gifts. Responsibility for self and acknowledgment of the achievement of others is part of this.

3] **Independence:** Without a sense of autonomy, we can become pawns in a world where others control our destiny. Individual freedom and self-management are to be nurtured. We need self-discipline to empower ourselves.

4] Generosity: Integrate autonomy with belonging. Success is to be shared by all, not just a special few. People who experience a feeling of Belonging, Mastery and Independence, are most likely to express Generosity.

Imagine the world we would have if everyone were to embrace these values. Every step we take to heal our Planet can be an act of self-healing. The reverse is also true.

Our world really does need more love. Tap into your compassion and create change where you believe it is needed.

Use your voice. Speak of the positive world you envision rather than of what you don't want. Transform negative energy into positive. We're all here waiting for you to shine your peaceful light in the world.

Janine (Jan) Moore is a Lifestyle Career Coach with over twenty years as a Career Counselor and Workshop Facilitator. She is devoted to creating a community of women who want to enjoy a New Economy Career that fits their lifestyles and allows them to experience Belonging, Mastery, Independence, and Generosity. Her recipe for a New Economy Career: Personal Meaning + Positive Social Impact + Community = Your New Economy Career.

www.WorkOnYourOwnTerms.com

LinkedIn: https://ca.linkedin.com/in/janinelmoore

PEACEFUL POINT by Kathie Tuhkanen

#Peace for the Mind of a Single Mom

The slightest glimmer of rays appear on the horizon, the sign of the coming dawn. It's barely past five in the morning but the young ones are restless and anxious to start their day. A heavy thud is heard as feet land on the floor and hasty footsteps get louder and louder. "**Mommy!** Time to wake up!" is the sound of my alarm and my only warning that I will be climbed over if I don't get up momentarily.

Barely able to open my eyes because somehow four hours of sleep just isn't enough to keep me going, I brace myself for the mountain climbing exercise about to take place. I am the mountain. There are two ways to look at this situation: either my son is trying to control my sleep pattern and should be sent away; or he's looking for creative ways of waking me so that we can spend a few extra minutes together.

I prepare for the mountain climber to make his way up and over the mommy bum mountain range so that he can be tickled and maybe even hugged after making his way safely onto the bed. I treasure these moments that would normally find me less than pleased, especially after seeing how quickly my eldest son has grown and the disappearance of his simple little adventures. He's no longer the young boy I still see him as. He's becoming more independent, not needing me as he used to. He hears the commotion and comes to investigate. After watching as his younger brother climbs up and gets tickled, he comes to the rescue and tickles me, so then it's two against one.

Fun moments like this were few and far between at one time. Thankfully, time and small fun moments have been able to help heal the rift in our family when their father and I separated. The boys alternate weekly between homes and they have been able to find solace in our family situation.

I asked both of them one day what they thought about our family situation, and the answer I received surprised me. They love having two homes; the idea that they have a broken home has never entered their minds. They have two parents who love them and two places to call home. In fact, they love the idea that they get to celebrate every holiday twice (except Christmas, when they get to celebrate three times because of getting together with extended family on their father's side).

I never thought of it in the way my boys did and in hearing that they love what has become a new normal for them has helped me find peace knowing that things are going to be just fine.

Kathie Tuhkanen is a Health & Wellness Life Coach and a Business Consultant specializing in nutrition and financial planning. She is very involved in the non-profit sector, offering various forms of support. Kathie is a loving mother, engaged in the local community, and making this world a better place.

Kathiej@live.ca

CHAPTER TWENTY-TWO by Jewels Rafter

Raising Vibrations to Find Your Inner Peace

For years, like many other people, I lived my life failing to understand that inner peace is actually a personal choice. I was often under the assumption that I had no control over what I was thinking, because I never considered the concept that thoughts can be altered and perspectives can be changed. So I consciously started to focus on my thoughts and I realized that much of what I was thinking did not accurately reflect the way I felt. Just by paying attention to them, I understood that many of my inner thoughts were actually fear-based and judgmental. I wanted to be released from all the conflict in my life, to remain unreactive to other people's words or actions, and to feel a sense of serenity within my soul. Therefore, it was crucial for me to alter or to stop the negative cycle of events which seemed to govern my relationships and my life, and find some inner peace again. How was I supposed to feel any tranquility in my heart when my emotions were fluctuating up and down according to what was happening inside my head or in my external environment? At this very point, I understood that we are vibrational creatures fueled by our thought patterns, and as such have the power to create peace within ourselves.

The easiest way to start creating inner harmony is to monitor your thoughts. The key to achieving a Zen state of mind is to simply accept what is happening in our lives. Knowing that only we ourselves can change our perceptions enables us to recognize ego's voice and offers us the opportunity to shift those negative thoughts into positive ones. There's a lot of negative energy and madness in this world, but we can all learn to live serenely. If your intention is pure and comes from deep within you, it will happen. On the outside, nothing changes exponentially; but by making simple shifts on the inside, peace of mind will eventually transpire.

By becoming more aware of who you really are, by knowing you are loved, by shifting the way you perceive, by practicing compassion and accepting your environment, you can initiate this tranquility process. As serenity and unconditional love fills your heart, you will have no desire to go back and will not relinquish what you have now found; an inner peace that you have been longing for your whole life. If we want to transform our reality and be free from problems, we must first learn how to transform our minds and our perceptions.

When things go astray in our lives and we encounter difficult or challenging times, we tend to regard the situation itself as the problem, but in reality the challenges we experience are created in our minds. If our response to difficulties are positive or peaceful, they will not be problems for us; it could even be possible to regard them as challenges or opportunities for growth and spiritual awakening. Difficulties arise when we react to situations with a negative frame of mind. So it is crucial to transform our minds in order to be free from problems. Worries, unhappiness, suffering, and pain exist within our thoughts; they are all unpleasant feelings, which are part of the mind. By acknowledging and cleansing our negative views, we can shift our mindset.

The energy that connects our entire universe is the same energy present within you. If you can raise the vibrational frequency of that energy, then your life can become more fulfilling, happier, and meaningful. How does one raise vibrations? Well it's easier than you may realize. When you raise your vibrational frequency you open the doors to abundance, bliss, and more happiness. You live and think in the positive vibration that you wish to exist on and as a result, you manifest all the marvels corresponding to that elevated energetic frequency.

Everything around us and everything that exists is made of energy: that food in your refrigerator, the flowers growing outside your house, even the computer you're using to search the web. When you view energy on a cellular level, you don't discover matter, instead you will see pure energy. Additionally, each of us has an individual aura that vibrates at its own unique vibrational frequency. So when you raise your vibrations, you directly affect your physical world.

We experience different levels of vibrations and energetic frequencies which are simply mental, emotional, and physical states of being. Consequently, our thoughts and feelings have different levels of vibrations. Negative emotions and thoughts such as jealousy, fear, resentment, anger, and despair vibrate at a very low frequency, while positive thoughts and feelings of delight, love, joy, and gratitude vibrate more rapidly and at a much higher frequency.

When searching for inner peace, it's crucial to understand that if you surround yourself with negativity, eat processed fast foods, or ingest lots of alcohol or drugs, then your energetic field turns hazy, dark, and blocked. Your vibrational levels are the key to attracting and manifesting your experiences. We are all responsible for the manner in which we choose to live on this planet, for the events we choose to experience, and for the choice to spiritually evolve and grow. We have more power to affect our reality more than we realize. By making positive choices and surrounding ourselves with empowering thoughts, we will begin to feel a sense of harmony and serenity.

So how can we begin this process? There are a few daily routines we can welcome into our lives to kick start the journey to happiness. An important habit is to practice unconditional self-love to boost your energetic makeover. The frequency of your energy vibrations depends immensely on self-love. Now, I understand that it can be very challenging at times to do this, especially if you made errors or poor choices in your past. Nonetheless, beating yourself up and listening to the negative chit-chat in your head is a habit that must be eliminated as soon as possible. With repetition, compassion, and empathy, you'll love yourself once again. Life can be challenging when you least expect it. If you make mistakes, don't be critical of yourself. Accept that you are only human and challenges will arise. Instead of getting frustrated, send yourself love and acceptance for learning the lessons in this school called life.

When trials arise, and they will, don't become the enemy, become an ally to your vibrations and thoughts. Be gentle and patient with yourself. Your mistakes are opportunities to learn and grow from where you are to where you want to be, in regards to vibrational frequency. Be aware that mistakes are opportunities to learn life lessons. These experiences help accelerate your development, so embrace them. You can be healed from the inside out using compassion, unconditional love for self, and forgiveness. Got to a place where you are gentle with your emotions and judgments. Be compassionate with yourself. Remind yourself of your own inner beauty, accept that you will have challenges, and sometime you may fail. However, it does not mean that it's necessary to let your vibrations plummet to the floor. Remain positive and fill yourself with light. This will raise your vibrational frequency that resonates with peace.

By simply becoming more aware, you will begin to develop your intuition and spiritual consciousness. Forgetting that you are a spiritual being is easy when social media bombards us with images of materialism and perfection. But if we really look at it, we are spiritual beings having a human experience. So better to make it a positive, high vibrating one! When you overlook the fact that we have many levels and are multidimensional creatures, our vibrational frequency can drop and slow down resulting in negative thoughts and feelings. See yourself as mind, body, and spirit, contrary to just skin and bones. Open up your energy bubble and feel the connection to the rest of the universe.

Another important factor in finding inner peace is to continue learning and reading. Keeping our minds open to new ideologies and thought patterns always raises your vibrations. Reading books that uplift your mood, that motivate, or inspire will help you to become the person you desire to be. Manifest the beauty you wish to see in the world, by bettering and empowering yourself with knowledge. When you transform your thoughts or your intentions, you raise the vibrational frequency of your spirit. As a result, this affects humanity as a collective.

Take time out to meditate, stop and connect with the universe once in a while. Through meditation and visualization, you can transform negative behaviors and increase your positive vibrational frequency. When you surround yourself with calmness and Zen energy, you have the ability to transform your thought patterns and limiting beliefs by simply visualizing and going to a happy place in your mind. This tells your subconscious that you are happy, thus raising your vibrations. Accepting that we are connected to the universe and expanding our consciousness results in a sense of inner peace. You're part of an enormous energetic ecosystem on earth and beyond. Matter is linked to you and constantly vibrating in various forms. The air you breathe, the water you drink, the earth you stand on, the flowers you grow, the animals you feed, the sunshine that warms you – all exist as one living consciousness that supports and sustains life on this amazing planet.

Develop an appreciation for all things big and small. Life is diverse. When you understand that no two things are alike, your appreciation for all creations intensifies. Be aware of that no two items fit in one specific category. It is crucial to be tolerant of the diversity here on earth and your energy should reflect that by participating in activities that resonate with your desires and vibrational frequency.

Remember that your thoughts are powerful – each and every one of them have a vibration of their own. Both positive and negative thoughts vibrate at different frequencies. Since humans are beings of energy as well, we have the power to create our reality with our thoughts. So if you are thinking positive, happy thoughts, you are creating a positive environment where everything flows freely. Whereas thinking negatively, or focusing on what you don't want will simply manifest it into your reality. You, dear friend, are a powerful creature. When you understand the innate power that your feelings, sensations, thoughts, and words possess, you will grow immensely and manifest your desires. Thus, creating a happy, positive environment. Inner peace will then have the opportunity to set in. This can only occur how-ever if you take control of those elements within you. If you constantly repeat negative thoughts towards yourself and others, you will create negative vibrational energy, which manifests as negative challenges and obstacles. Alternatively, if your thoughts are focused on the positive aspects in your life, then you will draw greater energy and manifest that which you desire.

Focusing on the natural beauty that surrounds you will also raise your vibrations. Take a moment to stop running and take a moment to appreciate, admire, and absorb the beauty that is all around you. Awaken your senses to the sights and sounds that nature blesses us with every day. Listen to the sound of the leaves rustling after a gentle wind, observe the twinkling stars in the night sky, or hear the song of a chickadee calling out to you. If you search for beauty using all of your senses, you will see that it exists everywhere. You simply need to appreciate it again with child-like wonder. Next time you're stressed and preoccupied with your issues, stop and take the time to notice the beauty around you. Embrace it, breathe in deeply, close your eyes, and really feel it. Become absorbed in that very moment of appreciation. This will allow you to feel a oneness with the universe.

One of the most important practices however, is to keep a daily gratitude journal to focus on appreciation. This is one of the very significant things you can do to achieve that sense of gratitude and inner peace. By focusing on the things you are grateful for, you will raise your vibrational frequency into a higher state. When your main and daily focus is gratitude, you highlight all that is already abundant in your life. As a result, you become appreciate and grateful. Gratitude raises your vibrations. I make it a habit to note all the things I am grateful for as soon as I wake up each morning. It sets the tone for a loving, high vibrational energy all around you and creates a day filled with positive thoughts. Often when we practice being thankful, we go through the process of counting our blessings, acknowledging the wonderful people, things, and places that make up our reality. While it is fine to be grateful for the good fortune we have accumulated, true thankfulness stems from a powerful comprehension of the gift of simply being alive, and when we feel it, we feel appreciative regardless of our circumstances. In this deep state of gratitude, we recognize the purity of the experience of being, in and of itself, and our thankfulness is part and parcel of our awareness that we are one with this great mystery that is life. It can be difficult for some of us to access this level of consciousness as we are very caught up in the fluctuations of our individual experiences in the world. The thing to remember about the world, though, is that it ebbs and flows, expands and contracts, gives and takes, and is by its very nature somewhat unreliable. Feel gratitude from deep within. Only then will it become true thankfulness.

Nowadays we are inundated with so much information from the media, social networks, our workplace, or even from home life. Our brains become frazzled and overworked regularly. This is why it is so imperative to learn how to mediate and quiet your mind. Clearing your mental chaos should be a priority on your daily "to do" list. Meditation is a state of serenity, calm and quiet. When you achieve a meditative state, you stop the continuous mental activities that lead to stress and restlessness in your life. The result: a state of consciousness and Zen energy. It's not necessary to sit crossed legged chanting "Om" for hours on end, but rather it's the simple process of stopping for ten minutes a day to change your vibrational frequency and alleviate stress. The best part about meditation is that it costs nothing and you will feel the benefits and a sense of inner peace almost instantaneously.

Another way to reinvigorate your nervous system is to learn how to breathe deeply. We forget how to breathe consciously from our diaphragm. Diaphragmatic breathing allows you to find a calm vibration, which raises your vibrational frequency as a whole. This type of breathing technique will have a positive effect on your entire nervous system, resulting in a continuous calm and tranquil state. Diaphragmatic breathing is a technique that is acquired with practice and consciousness. Essentially, it entails breathing large amounts of oxygen through your diaphragm and into your vital organs, instead of breathing shallow breaths from your upper chest. It does take some practice, however the rise in energetic frequency is well worth the effort. Breathing deeply will also send endorphins to your brain which sends you to that happy place in mere seconds.

Best-selling author Peter Voogd states that if you hang around with five confident people, you will be the sixth. This concept is basically founded on the idea that if you surround yourself with positive people who uplift and invigorate your spirit, you will reflect their vibrations. The reason this occurs is that your vibration raises or drops according to the strongest energy frequency in your proximity. If the frequency of someone is higher than yours, then your vibrational frequency vibrates faster. If it's lower, then your vibrational frequency slows down. I believe that it is crucial to surround yourself with people that uplift you. Happy, confident, awakened people will help you to remain in a positive state of mind. This means you energetic frequency will always be vibrating higher and you will feel contented and happy in whatever you choose to do. When you're conscious of your vibrations, you can sense when they're high or low. Furthermore, you can identify what causes the fluctuations you experience on a day-to-day basis. Your thoughts and surroundings directly affect your energetic frequency and vibrations.

Consequently, these fluctuations in frequencies rise or drop according to the frequency of the things around you. So make it a conscious choice to surround yourself with uplifting people, fill your mind with positivity and purpose, and send unconditional love to all those around you whether they deserve it or not. This practice will keep your vibrations high and energized at all times! By choosing kindness, we allow positive energy to flow all around us which prevents negative energy from reaching us or infusing our environment. By remaining in a state of conscious happiness, we create and maintain a connection to our higher selves which allows us to attain inner peace and contentment.

Inner peace is not something that is unattainable nor is it only available for a chosen few. It is a state of mind, an awareness of all the beauty that surrounds us and our appreciation and gratitude for it all. By focusing on these positive thoughts, by trying to better yourself and helping others, you will find that serenity and Zen state of mind. I encourage you to slow down, take in all the beauty and possibilities around you, and awaken your spirit to welcome happiness into your daily life. Only then will your awareness develop and allow inner peace to seep into your soul.

Jewels Rafter is an International Clairvoyant, Medium, Holistic Therapist, and Radio Show Host who has been living her passion for over fifteen years. She is the CEO of Harmony Radio and her own company, Ohm Readings & Therapies. She is a single mom of two beautiful teenage daughters who help to keep her grounded. Jewels specializes in Clairvoyant Readings, Mediumship, and holistic therapies. Her passion is to help people find answers and offer guidance by sharing her gifts. Having faced and overcome numerous personal challenges, she loves empowering women and helping them find their light at the end of the tunnel.

PEACEFUL POINT by Laura Haskell

#Peace is Within Your Heart's Home

Peace is within that place in our hearts we call home.

How many of you know where your home is?

When my marriage was stripped from me and my two children were bounced back and forth between my house and their father's house, I'm pretty certain they didn't have a strong sense of where their home was either.

Peace within is that comfortable place in our hearts where we fill joy on a daily basis. We feel safe and secure and we know without a doubt that we have some purpose in life. When you don't have peace within, you don't know where your home is.

The online definition of home is a dwelling-place used as a permanent or semi-permanent residence for an individual, family, household or several families in a tribe. So with that description, imagine peace within as a dwelling place – a home, that resides in your heart. If you could live in the best home, what qualities would it have? Would there be lots of Love? Forgiveness? Creativity? Joy? Safety? Openness? Stillness? Freedom? Confidence?

What does your home feel like?

I struggled for years not feeling satisfied, always looking outside of my home (my heart) grasping and wanting. I was still searching externally for my home for that something, or that someone, or that someplace that was going to make me feel whole and complete. For me, everything that was going to make me feel peace within, I was going to find it outside of myself. So I've spent years desperately soul-searching for satisfaction.

What happens when we do fulfill our longings? It often brings on more desires. This whole process can be very exhausting and feel empty.

There are two great disappointments in life: not getting what you want and getting it. The process of such unskillful desires can become an endless journey. Peace within comes not from fulfilling our wants but actually from the moment that dissatisfaction ends.

Many of us that enter into some kind of practice to heal our loneliness, depression, sorrow, or wounds end up realizing that a deep healing of our heart (our home) is necessary.

Even though many of us live through distancing ourselves from our physical state, we can still learn to live in our bodies because much of our somatic pain is a manifestation of emotional, mental, energetic, or spiritual holding patterns.

As Oscar Wilde put it, "It's not the perfect but the imperfect that we need to love."

Most often, to heal our hearts we must begin to open ourselves up to a lifetime's accumulation of acknowledged sorrow, both personal and universal.

So peace within is a daily practice of returning back home to our hearts. Are you ready to return to your heart?

Laura Haskell is the founder of Evolution Healing Center. She is a certified Mind Body Spirit Teacher, Medical Qigong Practitioner, Reiki Master, Angel Card Reader as well as many other energy medicine modalities. Laura helps people to return to their inner knowing by helping them to return to their hearts.

laura.haskell@yahoo.ca

CHAPTER TWENTY-THREE by Susan Mantz

Divine Peace, Love and Healing

You don't know me. You've never heard my story and quite frankly one chapter isn't enough to tell it all in. I don't know you and I don't know your story, but I can bet you a million stars in the sky that we are very similar in one way or another as are our stories. The way I see it is everything boils down to love or the lack thereof.

I'll share this part of my story with you and we'll go from there. I lost my twin granddaughters at their ages of eleven in a house fire and I lost my husband soon after. Along with the passing of my beloved husband, I also lost my home on Maui, all of our belongings, and so on and so forth. I could bore you with all the traumatic experiences I've endured, but why? I'd rather fill your minds with everything I've discovered to overcome them. First and foremost, let us begin by saying, "I am an overcomer"! Yes, you are too! We all are.

Within this chapter you will discover ways to overcome fear, anxiety, loneliness, unworthiness, heartache, pain, and how you play such an important role in all that is, all that is to be, and all that ever was. Often we close ourselves off to the possibility that things happen for a reason. There is always a reason behind an event and it's always for our best and highest good and the best and highest good of others. As I recognize that everything happens, always, for my best and highest good, even when it may not appear as such, I relax into the flow of it and release all negative thoughts and low energy feelings about it. Freeing myself from all resistance from the really great stuff that is constantly, steadily, already on the way to me now.

If you would daily write these words down, focus on them for just a few moments, and see how they make you feel, your days will get better and better and better. I know because it worked for me.

Clarity, Love, Appreciation, Relief

It's kind of like a magic potion that opens up a positive vibration and sets your mood in a better place every time you do it. With this, surrounding yourself with everything you find beautiful, makes you feel beautiful. Creating beauty also brings feelings of peace and love to your soul and lifts your spirits to a vibrational match of gratitude, self-worth, and happiness. I surround myself with quotes, poems, and inspirational pictures as well, some of which I'll share here with you. Daily, your life will take a turn for the better.

> *"We must exercise ourselves in the things which bring happiness, since, if that be present, we have everything, and if that be absent, all our actions are directed at attaining it."* Epicurus

> *"You are the light, an eternal flame. Your gift is your light, known by your name. You are the sun setting and rising every day. Your light never darkens, never goes away. You are the beam of energy, an energy not unknown. No need to return from where you've come from, you are always home."* Susan Mantz

By concentrating on the lack of something you are creating resistance, therefor it cannot come to you. By concentrating on the feeling of having it, you must acquire it. It is law.

Are you aware that 98% of what goes into your own mind comes from somewhere outside of yourself? If you can clear the clutter of the 98% of all the suggestions, comments, remarks, advices, opinions, revelations, observations, and discoveries spoken to and/or written to your brain and follow the 2% of intuition that you, yourself perceive to be true, right, and real for you, right now, you will change your life, in an instant.

Working beliefs involves first, determining what you believe and then finding the evidence of it that supports your creation. This is how to create a conscious blueprint for your own reality and your beliefs are the blueprint for your reality. Holding in recycles negative thoughts and actions and creates barriers that leads to boredom instead of the creation of love. Allowing feelings, thoughts, and emotions to flow in and out is the key to recovery in perfect harmony and balance.

Thoughts are things. Pay attention to your thoughts because your thoughts create your feelings and your feelings create the outcome. When my thoughts and feelings aren't in alignment with my desires, I find any way I can to shift them into a better place, a better perspective, like this poem which I refer to as a message of love from the universe to me.

> *"You speak to me as a nightingale sings in the soft breezes at night to the listening ear. You, close to me always, never far away. You come to me without notice or preparation at all. And I fall. You break the spell of darkness that shrouds my light from its glow. You ease the pains that I've accustomed myself to. You release the fear and allow me to breathe again as if the air were stifled before. You remain forever. You remain forever. You remain forever."* Author unknown.

I'm reflecting on a conversation I had with someone not so long ago. The discussion was on trusting universal source to provide any and all things into our existence. However, limited the opinion of the other conversationalist was, the object of the awareness that this being, if only for a short while in his life, had experienced the ground rule in the art of allowing struck my heart as awe-inspiring and literally brought tears to my eyes. It is my belief that once a person has opened the gift, which lays dormant in most due to what I call unauthorized suggestions by others, it remains in subconscious therefor always accessible regardless of how long one has failed to exercise the use of it.

It's easy to spot one who is self-fulfilled as opposed to one who is what I refer to as a "happy sponger". This is one who only receives temporary happiness by sucking the life out of those who have already found inner joy. Ironically, most people do this, only because they are unaware of how to obtain it themselves as of yet. They are the joy borrowers and when all is said and done, when the sponge has gone dry, they are left right back where they began because let's face it, borrowed joy is just that – borrowed. The trained soul can give a little, then walk away without allowing the happy sponger to drain them dry. How do I become a trained soul you ask? Easily, by finding and maintaining the peace that passes all understanding within. It is the awareness of the balance needed while both giving and receiving without overdoing it or being drained from it.

In all things, we need balance because balance creates harmony. All else is discord.

When we are saddened, we are also enlightened. When we are afraid, we are also strengthened. When we are alone, we are also aware. Everything has its purpose and balance, ready for us to recognize and expand from it.

Think of the balance of strength and softness within this poem:

> *"How then can I tell you of my love, strong as the eagle, soft as the dove, tall as the pine tree that stands in the sun and whispers in the wind you are the one."* Author unknown.

Releasing the need to control the outcome is also a very significant part of inner peace. When you are in a state of non-resistance to change, you are also in a state of allowing, and in that state of allowing, every good possible thing can and will easily flow to you.

Just as an author writes a script for an actor to play a role in a movie, you also have this same power to create whatever life you desire by writing, or even rewriting, your own script. Universe will then provide you with the people, places, and things needed for your new life to then begin. I purposely did this often, and still do today. The written word has power in it because the intention is set into action through your focused attention to it while writing.

There is no right or wrong in where you are or what you are experiencing. There is awareness, growth, and expansion of self. With this acknowledgment, this light, comes the peace that passes all understanding along with comfort in the now and positive expectations for the future.

The one constant is change. We are never alone. Everything is connected. Energy flows where attention goes. Love is the strongest and highest form of energy. To love oneself is to have it all and then some.

"When old upsetting memories are being released some of the greatest days in your life are ahead."

This is how I'm finding peace. Join me.

Susan Mantz is a Home Health Care provider for a family member fighting, and winning, a battle with lymphoma and blindness. She is an entrepreneur with over twenty-five years of intuitive tarot reading experience and inspires those led to her. In high school, Susan was awarded a letter for her vocal talents.

PEACEFUL POINT by Troy Smith

#Peace – Humanity's Journey

Peace...Peace...Peace. Just saying the word brings a state of calm. It allows your whole body to breathe and fills itself with the joys of the spirit. Just take a deep breath and say the word as you exhale three times. Feel that? It's your spirit aligning with your source. Peace is the unspoken goal of all living beings. No matter what external goals may be, peace is what it all boils down to.

Through the misguided actions of "New World" settlers, the heartless attempted extermination of whole races of people, or the multi-generational wars over single strips of land, all of these people ultimately sought what they believed to be peace. The further understanding and acceptance of true peace would eliminate all of these actions which brought the opposite known as chaos.

Harming another in any way can never bring peace. Peace can only be achieved through love and acceptance.

There is an ancient story of a Chinese mentor considered to be the wisest in the land and was one of the teachers of Confucius. War broke out in his homeland. So disgusted by it, he decided to leave and find a place where he could continue to practice and experience peace. As he approached the guard at the gate, the guard stated that he would not let him leave until he recited to him the secrets of life. The teacher then proceeded to recite eighty-one verses of what became known as the Tao Te Ching. The book is widely considered to be the definitive work on establishing a flourishing society and happy life. This work predates the Christian bible and sums up the meaning of life to be a search for, and practice of, peace.

When we practice peace, which is an internal state of being, all things become joyous. From birth to transition and every moment in between, peace allows for true love and appreciation to exist for all. Ultimately, it comes down to the single truth of we and not "us and them." Peace, love, and a joyous life can only be achieved by embracing our oneness. Anything that falls short of this ultimate truth can only bring further chaos and pain. Peace is the ultimate goal of the spirit.

If ever you run into someone who just seems to be determined to bring hate or chaos, take the time to learn what it is that they are afraid of. Hate is a by-product of fear. They fear that they may not be able to achieve their peace if another gets what they desire. They are living from a place of lack and not from a place of abundance. If we were to bring this person love and acceptance, the hate would cease to exist and peace would reign supreme.

Troy Smith is a Coach, Consultant, Speaker, and Trainer whose focus is to help others discover the power within themselves. He has spent the last thirty-plus years in corporate and private industry management. During those years, he has been consistently tasked with building effective and productive teams. To facilitate that, he has studied coaching, psychology, spirituality, and systems extensively.

CHAPTER TWENTY-FOUR by Diana Alli D'souza

Peace – Touch Me Like the Feather of a Dove

I pay close attention to the presence of peacefulness touching the core of my soul like the feather of a white dove, symbolic of new beginnings, joy, peace, harmony, fidelity, and love. I am in awe with life in a space that prompts me to be still, quiet, and focusing on the here and now. No thoughts of past or future in these simple and humble surroundings as I settle myself and all my undertakings to the bare minimum – one small bedroom and a kitchen. The clutter, imaginary and physical, are left behind.

I have settled in Rishikesh, India, to do outreach to the most marginalized Indigenous populations. I return each year to this picturesque landscape cradled along the splendid banks of the sacred Ganges. Mother Ganga (the Gateway to the Himalayas) is the feminine embodiment and divine flow of consciousness. Her mythical essence is non-judgmental, accepting all who submit themselves into her sacred arms. Rishikesh is also called the Yoga Capital of the World. People from all over the world, all walks of life and faiths come together to experience the Divine within them and look for the Divine in others: sages, philosophers, and gurus. People come in droves searching for enlightenment. All along its course of the Ganges, Hindus bathe in its waters, paying homage to their ancestors and to their gods. Wherever you go, be it a temple, ashram, or shrine, it will draw you to join a Satsang (being in the company of the truth or the good by sitting together with a guru or a group of spiritual students), or soak in the simplicity of native life. This is my fourth trip to this magnificent yet modest part of the world, opening my senses towards peace and fulfillment. I am in balance, letting go of all that tormented me in my past. I am in an aura of my own, spiritually connected to my higher being, feeling free at last.

As I reflect on my own passage through time, there have been rough patches. The loss of my dear father in a fire accident; soon my only brother at nineteen years of age (eleven months my junior) died tragically, accidentally thrown off a moving train. My mother, who suffered chronic mental illness, left my dad and three young children (I was ten years old then) without a goodbye (I brought her back into our lives [with my then younger sister] in my early twenty's). I ran away twice in my life from two unstable situations: an aunt with a brain aneurysm (did not know it then) in the UK, and an abusive marriage that ended in Canada. I can relate to Kubler Ross' five stages of grief model: denial, anger, bar-gaining, depression, and acceptance. We all deal with a heaps of stuff. I had no other choice but to come to terms with acceptance – move on or sabotage the rest of my life with misery addiction! I made a pact with myself that I would have to get rid of my insecurity blanket fast. My children needed to live happier and more fulfilling lives. I had to reassure them that they were blameless in this complex turn of events. I soon found courage to build confidence and strength in myself and in turn, pass it on to them. I lucked out with my generous employer rescuing me from my unfortunate plight with financial and moral support. The rewards of working tirelessly throughout my career, especially in the time of despair, paid dividends. My colleagues and friends were a bridge extending their arms to help me cross over troubled waters.

Losing so much as a young single mother and woman, my faith in God became my pillar of strength to lean on. His Divine intervention through the healing process opened doors and many wonderful new opportunities. Healing meant I had to forgive in order to move on, and so I made absolution with those who caused me great sorrow. Releasing myself of karmic debt made me more spiritually prepared to face the rest of the journey ahead of me. I often use the peace prayer by St. Francis of Assisi as my guidepost, *"Make me a channel of peace, where there is hatred - love,.. injury – pardon... doubt – console, understand, love...In giving to all...that we receive..."* Yes, it took a while, but I have learned over the years that no matter how right or wrong you are, and I know it is the toughest act of admission, apologizing can heal and release immense burdens placed on the troubled mind and fragmented soul. It can turn us into heroes of grace and integrity. Pressing the delete button does not erase the memory, it is still there, but its harshness has faded away. Peace awaited me like an anchor, readily available whenever I opened myself to witness its unconditional preparedness to enter and rest with me.

My fate ahead was a promising one. The senior team in a university setting saw true potential in me and charged me with building a centre that focused on improving academic and personal well-being through initiatives and extracurricular pursuits in and out of the classroom, locally, nationally, and internationally. In addition, my work has led to establishing more than two dozen programs for disadvantaged and underrepresented students and communities: tutoring and mentoring programs, outreach to isolated seniors and the homeless (including launching a student-run homeless clinic with support from faculty in the health science), global outreach – books to fill libraries in war torn countries, and benefit concerts (music, dance) pertaining to health and well-being for destitute children. Our contributions to civic engagement resulted in immeasurable accomplishment and success. Threading in what was already in my treasure box, gems of generosity, joy in helping others through compassion, altruism, and social responsibility, led to gratification of the soul; selflessly spreading joy so that others could bask in its sparkle and shine.

Life has an interesting way of teaching us many lessons; there are many forks on the road less traveled. I have set foot on numerous turns and twists around the bend and made mistakes along the way. The risks taken opened endless opportunities and added many accolades and distinctions to my portfolio. *"I can't change the direction of the wind, but I can adjust my sails to always reach my destination."* James Dean. The course has inevitable changes, the unpredictable winds certainly teach us unique lessons to face adversity with toughness, grit, and perseverance, realizing there might be storms that may undoubtedly arise. If so, my sail is ready to be readjusted.

My newfound passion through Access Empowerment Council, a foundation I started four years ago, has led to empowering children globally, providing needy resource to ashrams and NGOs. I now teach English to marginalized Indigenous children and youth in India. Who would have thought I would trek thousands of miles away, all alone to a distant part of the world inspiring young lives and instilling confidence in their personal and academic journeys. I work in the poorest surroundings making a difference in the lives of young students with bare necessities eagerly waiting to break the poverty cycle for their families and themselves.

Like a caterpillar, I have emerged from my cocoon morphing into a glorious butterfly earning my wings to freedom. I am now a positive force to reckon with. I count my many blessings and accept with gratitude the lessons learned from the storms that swept me to new pastures, bringing a joyful, peaceful, and transformative presence in my awakened soul. I thank God most of all for being my compass and strength throughout my journey. As tough as it may have been, it has paved its way to supporting others going through their own personal ordeals. Six decades later, I can feel peace touching my soul with her blessed presence.

I still have a long way to go to impact this world through philanthropy and humanitarianism. I am reminded of a mantra to keep me going. The advice I give myself to stay on track with the next stage of my journey, comes from the words of William Penn, the famed Quaker philosopher who said, "I will walk this way but just once and any good I can do let me do it now, let me not forget, defer or neglect it for I will never pass this way again! Life is limitless, until my feet can take me no more. I know that my mind (hopefully sane by then) will have the power to move mountains!"

A passionate trailblazer on Social Responsibility, Diana Alli D'souza has founded/co-founded and facilitated nationally recognized outreach programs in the Faculty of Medicine, University of Toronto. Through Utihp.ca she has raised tens of thousands of dollars for destitute children around the globe. Diana has served on numerous Boards: Governing Council, community foundations, local/national committees. She is the recipient of 12 MD graduation awards, University Awards, numerous University of Toronto awards, the prestigious Order of Ontario and the Queen Elizabeth II Diamond Jubilee Medal, and community recognition.

PEACEFUL POINT by Mary Hilty

#Peace and Persistence

There is a lovely little place just inside of ourselves where we can feel our lives are of importance. We create it so that the things causing anger, pain, fear, and anxiety can be filed neatly away, where they cannot control the essence of our lives. We bring everything we are from a particular place inside ourselves, and I believe that place is called the Kingdom of Peace.

In the Kingdom of Peace, we share our lives joyously, unashamedly, and fearlessly. We know that what we do and say to improve the quality of another's life powerfully elevates that other life. Good people do this without thought...great people do it without any conscious effort at all. Humans beings have the unique ability to see outside of themselves and reach into pain felt by others. We have the capacity to soothe, comfort, and encourage people and walk with them into the light of beautiful peacefulness.

We live in such a time of violence, uncertainty, greed, and unrest. What is different about now compared with time gone before is that currently we have an amazing way we can reach out to anybody and make our circle of influence better, safer, happier, and stronger – people everywhere benefiting from people everywhere. And all that is necessary is truthful, open, honest, forthright communication. Humanity goes "off track" from time to time. Priorities become skewed and self-importance seems at the heart so many issues. Yet, there are those of us who will gather together and march with strength and purposefulness away from the clatter that can wound us so deeply. We are warriors...each and every one of us...reaching into our Kingdom of Peace and building ties of love and truth. If we do this in our circle of influence and it grows outward as circles do...then guess what we have done? We have created Warriors for Peace!

Mary Hilty has written extensively through journaling, composing poems, and a variety of articles. She considers her social interactions with people to be one of her greatest inspiration for writing, which she has been doing most of her life. A favorite dream is to co-create with other authors and leave her "best self" in the world through writing!

CHAPTER TWENTY-FIVE by Jennifer Martel

The Journey to Peace Through Transformation

You are in your early twenties and you make a bad choice that results in a criminal record. You go through the next few years of life trying to forget about what happened and try to get back on your feet. You send out your resume to hundreds of job postings and are fortunate to get several interviews. However, you're unable to pass a background check. You are passed over for yet another job you're qualified to do because they won't give you a chance to prove yourself. You are mad at yourself and depressed that you just cannot get ahead.

Many people cannot empathize to the challenges a person faces having a criminal record. In fact, only 5.75 percent of the population, or just over two million Canadians, can speak about it firsthand.

People without a criminal record are quick to judge, often saying that someone with a "record" is just simply a bad person. Canada is the only country in the world with a systematic method of clemency. This allows the individual a second chance by sealing their criminal record. I believe we should have faith in humanity and allow people the peace within themselves to be good citizens. We all make mistakes at some point in life and we should have the opportunity to show that it does not define our true character.

I grew up in a loving middle class, two parent home in the suburbs. My mom was a stay-at-home mother and my father was the breadwinner. I very rarely saw my parents fight and they worked very hard to give my brother and I everything they could afford. They lived within their means and were great role models. I never had any trouble with the police and cannot imagine what it might be like to be arrested and the shame it brings to one's self and their family. I would have never thought growing up that I would impact so many lives by just being kind and doing my job.

As a young girl, my dream was always to be a flight attendant. As I got older, I flip-flopped with my career choice but it always seemed that I would be a "people helper" in some way. My career took off in the travel industry and I became a travel agent. It was rewarding helping my clients book their travel arrangements and see a dream turn into reality with my help. I was always delighted to hear about their wonderful experiences. I got married, started a family, and my focus became my children. Working full-time while raising them was tough to balance. For several years I was a stay-at-home mom dedicating my life to my kids. While I was at home, I was introduced to the behind the scenes of helping others in the vulnerable position of having a criminal record. I helped out with the paper work associated with the record suspension (pardon) application process.

When it was time to return to the work force I had to find a balance; something flexible that would allow me to be present for my three children, but also contribute financially to the household. I embarked on a new career path becoming a Digital Fingerprint Technician. It was a natural fit with our family business, gave me the flexibility for my family's needs, and also the ability to be a pivotal contributor at the crossroads in someone's life. Fingerprints are the first step in sealing one's criminal record and getting a fresh start. As a Digital Fingerprint Technician, I was not only the person coming to take someone's fingerprints for their record suspension (pardon) application, but I was the individual giving that person some hope and reassurance things could be done to bring them down a new path for the future. You see, having a criminal record is not only a road block to employment but a personal struggle knowing that someone may be judged on a mistake they made in the past. It can be embarrassing to most individuals because it's not who they are today.

I found myself fingerprinting the most vulnerable people: the single mother on social assistance, the father that grew up in the projects that just wanted to do right by his children so they would not follow in his footsteps, and the people that just wanted a fresh start without judgment. I provided a mobile service, so I was able to meet my clients at their home where they were the most comfortable. Many of them felt hopeless and shared with me how they got to where they were.

Many of those stories were heart-breaking. It gave me a different perspective on other human beings – a "do not judge unless you can walk a mile in their shoes" approach. This allowed me to be open-minded and listen without judgment. Many of the clients remarked how easy it was to share and they did not feel judged. That sure was a nice feeling to hear.

Here are several reasons shared with me on how clients got to this point in their lives. Sometimes it was a crime of opportunity; other times it was being at the wrong place at the wrong time. It was fueled by anger or addictions, and sadly, it happened because of revenge or greed. It's about making a bad decision on any given day, regardless of the reason.

- They grew up with a drug addicted parent and were forced to step up as the caregiver to their sibling and had to steal food so they could eat.
- They were in a neglected relationship and to get attention, they would shoplift to force their partner to interact with them.
- They grew up in subsidized housing. To fit in or be part of the cool group, they would commit violent offenses as part of gang initiations.
- They would commit crimes so they would go back to jail because they just didn't know how to function in society.
- They had a drug addiction and would steal anything and everything to sell for their next fix.
- They were abused as a child and do not know how to react in a healthy relationship. They found themselves being controlled by their partner and ended up in a life of prostitution.
- They couldn't control their temper and they assaulted someone.
- They got involved in a scheme and stole money from their employer hoping they could fix their problem.
- They had too many drinks in a bar and thought they felt fine to drive home.
- They got pulled over for speeding and when the police searched their car, a small quantity of drugs were found.
- They got involved selling drugs and found out how profitable it was. Why work an honest job for minimum wages when they could make quick cash.

One thing is clear to me: not everyone with a criminal record is a "bad person."

Unfortunately, the journey to clemency is long and the criteria is stringent. The government must be certain that the person does not pose a danger or threat to the public by having their criminal record sealed. In 2012, the Federal Conservative Government made changes to this process in their "tough on crime" overhaul. An individual must demonstrate a law-abiding behavior for a minimum of five or ten years, depending on their crime. They must have completed their sentence, paid all fines/restitutions in full, and pose no risk to reoffend. They must not put the system of justice in disrepute. They must also pay a significant government processing fee and can take approximately eighteen to twenty-four months to complete. Often times, the individual is caught between the necessity of the record suspension (pardon) and the economic reality of not being able to afford the fees associated with it.

What is most rewarding about my profession is the privilege of seeing the transformation and rebirth of my clients from their lowest points, feeling hopeless, and giving them encouragement of what's to come. It's also about sharing with them their progress and seeing the excitement and hopefulness for the next step. And finally, it's calling them with the amazing news that their record suspension (pardon) has been granted. The feeling they have of peace and optimism for what they can now accomplish is beyond words. They sky really is the limit for them now and they're so grateful that someone was by their side on this journey.

I often times receive phone calls from past clients telling me how they are doing, that they are now employed, and their self-esteem is blossoming from all the opportunities they have received since sealing their criminal record. The greatest reward for me is getting a referral. They are confident in my ability to transform the life of their friend or loved one, providing someone else with the opportunity of finding personal peace.

The way I am able to attain inner peace for myself every night is by never compromising my personal integrity, always maintaining honesty and transparency with my clients, and allowing my personal growth to continue through my ability to help others transform their lives. I am a firm believer that people come into your life for a reason. Although these individuals are coming to me for "business" reasons, my clients have also taught me to be thankful for what I have in my life.

The world is so full of judgment and conflict these days. I feel that a little kindness, patience, and guidance can go a long way to making this world a better place. It makes me happy that I can bring a little bit of peace into the lives of people who once felt so hopeless.

Jennifer Martel is the owner and CEO of Pardon & Waiver Experts / On the SPOT Fingerprinting Services since 2009. She is certified by the Royal Canadian Mounted Police (RCMP) to process and submit digital fingerprints to the Canadian Criminal Real Time Identification services (CCRTIS). She has also been a legislative advocate for individuals with a past criminal record and has built awareness regarding criminal record suspensions (pardons) and US entry waivers. She is a married mother of three that enjoys scrapbooking, card making, baking, and relaxing with her family. She is dedicated to helping others with kindness, respect, and without judgment.

www.pweservices.com

www.facebook.com/PardonWaiverExperts

PEACEFUL POINT by Anna Jacono Paveling

#Peace Through the Seasons

Spring and Easter approaches as I put my pen to the notebook to reflect on what peace means to me. It brings to mind the smiling chocolate covered faces of my daughters from the egg hunting and years gone by. Those moments remind me of the warmth in my heart that I feel as I silently acknowledge that the four of us are together, healthy and blessed to witness the birth of a new season while we devour the sweets. Later in the month, the patio chairs are dusted off, and as I am wrapped in a cozy sweater, I read my book outside listening to the odd peep of the birds and smelling the garden soil as it warms in the sun. I am enveloped in peace.

I find peace as the summer meanders in as I place myself near water. The Credit River pushes by close to my neighborhood and I feel stress and tension easing from my body as I walk by the river bank, listening to the trickles and burbles along the way. Sometimes I throw bread to the ducks, watching them squabble over the pieces, and I try to throw extra to the slow one placed at the rear. As I sit on a beach alongside Lake Erie while camping with a friend, it affords me that same peace. Clean air, clean water, the sounds of waves; contentment!

As the leaves change and fall enters Ontario, it takes me back to my childhood. I relive the feelings of happiness and security while walking in conservation areas with my mother, picking up fallen chestnuts and examining leaves as perfect works of art. The smell, the color, and the crunch of the leaves wrap me in a peacefulness that I find hard to explain.

Winter with its long months and frigid temperatures is my least favorite season, but even within it are glimmers of peace. Certainly Christmas time, which means family time, is full of tranquil moments that I adore. I would be neglectful to not acknowledge that watching the Christmas lights shine on our tree with my husband beside me, sipping a glass of wine, and enjoying the colors is lovely and calming indeed. The closest times that spill over with inner peace are in the incredible diamond sparkle of a new snow in the park where I walk my dogs, and perhaps in the squeak of my boots as I tromp on a snow laden sidewalk, my feet toasty warm in my boots and my cheeks cold-kissed red.

In a world that sorely needs peace, there is pleasure and comfort in knowing that within each season, there are things that can bring peace to us all. We just need to look.

Anna Jacono Paveling is a wife, mother of two beautiful young women, and a Registered Nurse specializing in critical care. She enjoys walking the family dogs, and musicals of all kinds! She believes strongly in advocating for those without a voice and then giving warm, compassionate, and dignified care at the end of life.

Anna Paveling@APaveling

CHAPTER TWENTY-SIX by Sandi Chomyn

Healed By a Hug

I was in a foster home from the time I was an infant. Looking back, there was a mixture of good and bad experiences.

Up to the age of seven I did not realize or know I was in foster care, until I was told I was moving to a new home and new people that would be looking after me. It was just me moving on, nobody else. Suddenly, I had the sense of uncertainty and confusion. I felt very scared and alone for the first time in my life. It made me think I had done them wrong and they did not want me anymore. I was the bad child.

This new foster mom showed me all of the things she thought and felt I needed to know about household chores. I learned about cleaning, cooking, laundry, and gardening and was given an education. She told me these were things I needed to know when I was older and would be on my own in the world. I was there until I got married. At the time it was an escape to get away, as I felt I couldn't make it on my own.

As long as I can remember from an early age, things were always very impersonal in both foster homes. Not knowing any different at the time, I thought it was normal. Even though I saw things were different in other people's lives, I did not question it.

At a young age did I realize I was learning about different emotions? In my own way I most likely did but did not recognize them the same as others may have or should have or could have. My classmates called me retarded and teased me about being a foster child. I was always told by my foster parents and teachers that I would not amount to much of anything, because in their eyes they assumed I did not care or was a difficult child and student. In response I felt like nobody cared about me. I felt I was never good enough in their eyes. I was doing, so I thought, all of the right things or the things they were teaching me to do, but I still felt that they were judging me. Even though I had done everything that I was supposed to do and was told to do. This made it more difficult for me to understand what was going on in my life. This in turn made me defiant as I felt that is what they wanted.

As I was getting older, I was starting to recognize things within myself with mixed feelings. There were many emotions I had that totally confused me. I started comparing myself to others and noticed that I was "different," and my perception of what I felt was normal was starting to make me ask questions. But the questions were only in my own mind, as I felt I should not or could not talk about it. And in reality, at the time, I felt I had no one to turn to.

It was important to know what was happening in my life. I needed and wanted someone to explain the situation to me in a way that I could understand, someone I could trust and talk to about things. But I never had that, and then just pulled away in many ways.

In my late teens I was assigned a new social worker. When she came for scheduled visits, she took time with me. Suddenly, my opinions were important to someone. There were times she even asked me for advice. It was the very first time in my life that anyone seemed interested in me and my opinion. It helped me to start feeling confident in myself and to see that I had important things to share. She understood my needs, abilities and capabilities. We worked together on my school work, and together we built up my self-esteem. I started to be proud of who I was and know I was a beautiful person. The relationship with my social worker provided me with stability and helped me to feel less afraid. I didn't change overnight. It was and still is an ongoing growth. Maybe that social worker is reading this right now. I would like to say thank you as I did not get a chance back then.

She had moved on to new things in her life.

My biggest turning point was a lesson learned from my fiancé's mother. I had gone to the city with my future husband to go shopping and to the summer fair for the day. We then went over to his parents' for the evening meal and for a visit. As we were getting ready to leave and chatting at the door my fiancé's mom reached out and gave him a big hug. As I was standing there waiting to go she turned to me and enveloped me in a big hug that had me in shock. I had never been hugged like that before. I stood there not knowing how to act or feel about it. Yes I had been hugged by my boyfriend, but never from anyone else.

My fiancé's mom felt there was something missing when I didn't return the hug the same way she had given it. She looked at her son and asked what was wrong in her native tongue. Her son wasn't sure what to say. They both looked at me for an answer, which I wasn't sure I could give them.

Without saying much as it was an awkward situation, we let it go. I didn't though. I did a lot of thinking about it the next few days and weeks. I had a lot of mixed feelings about it because I wasn't someone who would talk about it, I internally processed it.

Days and weeks passed and I was to visit my fiancé's parents again. I still felt intimidated and unsure. We had our visit and were getting ready to go. Standing at the door my fiancé's parents gave him his hugs and "I love you." I was standing there waiting. When they were done; instead of them reaching

out to me, I reached out and gave both of his parents a hug. I thanked my fiancé's mother for teaching me something special that day of the fair. I then explained to them that I didn't receive hugs growing up, and that it was something new for me. She asked me why I had never been hugged. I told her what I only knew. I mentioned that I was a foster child and that they never showed the emotion to me like they did to their own children. Saying to her, somehow in my mind I thought it was normal but down deep knew it wasn't normal to even think the way I did. She said, "That was so wrong." We talked more about it through the years. For opening up to her I was wrapped in the arms of a hug by my fiancé's mother.

This was the start of many more hugs and "I love you's" to come.

My fiancé, at the time, also taught me someone did care about me and that I was more than good enough in their eyes. He always told me I am capable of doing anything I want and being the person I want to be. Through his love and understanding and not judging me, I have become that person. I have taught my own children that these two things are very important. They do not leave without receiving and giving hugs and saying "I love you." All phone calls are ended with "I love you." Yes, I do work at it continuously. I am very happy to say I have been now been married for over forty years and now have an endless supply of hugs!!

After reading these experiences, there may be things that you may have wished were different in your life. You can have it. Things can be overcome and changed. A lot you probably have had to learn on your own, even how to show different peaceful emotions in many ways.

So many foster children go through life wishing for more, and accepting just enough. Appreciate that love will always find you once you have peace and that you're also ready to be loved.

Sandi Chomyn is an International Best-Selling Co-author and Life Coach known as a Life Management Coach. After raising her three boys, she received her coaching training with Coaching Cognition. She's a farm mom and grandma, inside and out, and has come to enjoy the different facets of her life by integrating her life coaching business and her love for scenic photography with good country living. Sandi resides with her husband Bill in a small farming community in Togo, Saskatchewan Canada.

facebook.com/meetsandichomyn

facebook.com/sandichomyn

CHAPTER TWENTY-SEVEN by Anita Sechesky

Peaceful Spirit

The human spirit is so magnificent. It is the connection to the human mind and body and it even has the capacity to connect with other human beings. This is why peace is so powerful. We empathetically feel the emotional pain or trauma another person has lived through. I believe that peace is such a powerful energy that it causes our spirits to become connected as one. I am a strong believer that our spirits live forever and that love and peace are significant factors because of it.

For this chapter, I would like to share my own personal experience when I had lost my first child. My daughter was full-term and she was a perfect baby. There were no complications during the entire pregnancy that made us question anything. However, we did lose our beautiful little girl due to unforeseen causes. Yet, I had known instinctively something was not right and felt it within my spirit. I asked my doctor if I could be induced to have her delivered two weeks early. My obstetrician's office was over two hours away from my home. He decided not to interfere with the natural birth process that was planned since there wasn't any cause for concern at this point. When I went to the Emergency Department in a small northern community I was always told by the nurses that everything was fine, even though my baby's heart rate was lower in comparison to earlier assessments in my pregnancy. This occurred before I became I officially became a Registered Nurse and deeply disturbed me, as I already had some medical knowledge from other experiences at that time.

My pregnancy loss with my daughter was the most heartbreaking thing I have ever endured. No one from the hospital from my home community offered any support, nor the larger facility where I gave birth. Sadly, the loss of my baby was not the first one in these Northern communities

I tried to tell the nurses so many times that something was not right, but no one took me seriously. I must have gone to the Emergency Department at least a dozen times and was always told that I was over-thinking or something to that effect. The last time I went to Emerg, the staff finally took me seriously and put a stress monitor on me. All the previous times I went in, the stress monitor was being used or I was just sent home. I was never given the option to wait for the monitor to confirm my concerns.

As it turned out, my precious baby girl was stillborn and I had to deliver her on a maternity ward during the Christmas holidays, just two days before my own birthday. It was heart-wrenchingly painful to see the other mothers and their live babies.

The night before my induction, my daughter, Jasmine Rose's, sweet baby spirit came to me and before I knew it, I was hovering above looking down at my husband lying next to my lifeless body. I saw how my hands were folded across my pregnant belly with my daughter's body still within my womb. I remember looking at how beautiful and bright she was and then, just like that, I got caught up in the instantaneous rapture of leaving my physical body. Then as I was traveling upwards into the heavenly realms with my daughter, I remembered what my mom had just moments earlier spoken to me about, and I looked back down at my husband sleeping. She said that I should remember how much he loved me, and that we would have more children one day. The very moment that thought flashed through my mind, I was back inside my physical body and looking at my hands folded in front of me.

This experience left me realizing that death is only a transition and not a physical effort at all. In fact, my experience was completely effortless and merely a shift out of my physical body into my spiritual body. I believe that we already have our spiritual body inside of us and when we no longer need our physical bodies, we simply leave it behind.

However you may want to analyze it, I can say this was a profound and powerful revelation that gave me confirmation of life after death. How amazing to know that we never actually die or lose ourselves, but we are intact in our thoughts even after our physical bodies stop working! This is why I am a strong believer in my Christian faith. I choose to believe that I will be reunited with my loved ones and even embrace my baby girl once more in my arms.

I have learned that our spirit man is the essence of who we are. This concept is so profound that it can help us to become stronger in this life if we allow ourselves to accept that nothing is impossible, and that all is possible if we believe.

Yes, the human spirit is powerful and I can even tell you an experience I had with one of my pets. When our dear family pet died, it was a hard time for all of us, as our doggie girl was part of our family for over 13 years. She was like our first child and she was well loved within our community by our friends and family. I will never forget that following the first Mother's Day service after we had lost our beloved daughter, Jasmine Rose, our pet dog "Sandi" came into the bedroom and looked at me crying as I was curled up on my bed. She jumped up and snuggled right against my belly, as if someone had coaxed her to do that. She stayed there for a brief moment, jumped down, looked at me, and then walked away. When our beloved Sandi passed away at my parent's home, it was devastating because we never had a chance to say good- bye to her. The following day, I was sitting in my glider rocking chair just thinking that I never had a chance to tell her how much I loved her. All of a sudden, out of nowhere, I literally felt this amazing rush of energy. It was like a swift breeze. Before I knew it, our Sandi, in her spiritual form, sitting right next to my feet. Then automatically I felt my spirit man lean down and pat her, and my spirit within said, "Good girl." I couldn't believe this was happening and excitedly told my husband that I got to say goodbye to our pet. He was so happy and never doubted me because of the supernatural experiences I already had.

My reason for sharing these events is to help you realize that our spirit is something that we all contain within us. There is no explaining it. I believe from the time our cells are conceived and start vibrating, we are created in peace out of pure love and positive energy as we are all perfect creations by God within this Universe and all its glory. There is no need to fear the fact that our spirit is something that is unexplained. In fact, I believe in some special way if we embrace our lives differently, we may be exposed to more infinite possibilities that we would never have realized were always around us anyway. Many people already know that GOD is a spirit, as we cannot see HIM, yet we believe HE exists around us. Be open minded to what our Creator has created within you. You are unique and wonderfully made. Never doubt the endless possibilities of your peaceful human spirit. This life is but a journey and we are all headed in the same direction. Let's move forward in peace.

As you already know, my intention for this book is to help you see how we are all connected in the spirit of peace We don't have to personally know each other to understand life's hardships, trauma, and pain. Our unity as individuals simply believing in the common good creates a connection within our spirits. Can you imagine so many people across the globe equally realizing the need to reach out and show more empathy, compassion, and love for those around them? The human spirit ignited in love and peace will unite many. God is Love. Have you connected with Him as yet? It's all about relationship, not rituals. Just like any other relationship, start with introducing yourself. HE accepts you just as you are. Maybe it's time you do the same. Healing will become one of the benefits from this relationship. It all starts with you wanting more for yourself. The human spirit is one of the most beautiful gifts we have been given. It has unlimited possibilities.

Many times we may face extreme difficulties in our lives. When all hope is lost, what do you do? Do you have a support system? Not everyone does. It is a sad reality in this big world. Lives are changed instantly as a result of either good or bad experiences. When you carry pain deep within your heart, it affects the vibrancy of your life. Maybe it's time to start associating with positive people. Discover what your life's passions are by searching deep within your soul. You can begin your own healing right now, right where you are.

CHAPTER TWENTY-EIGHT by Anita Sechesky

Peace Always Attracts Love

Let me tell you, one of the most common trends I hear about is the fear of commitment when I coach people. Many of my clients have expressed this since everything around them is moving at such a rapid pace, and it seems that relationships are expected to move at the same speed. I have coached so many men and women who are struggling with whether they are ready or not for true love. Many times, we get so busy in our lives with routines and responsibilities that we put aside our longing to be accepted and loved by another person. It doesn't matter who you are and what you do for a living, you have every right to love and be loved. Unfortunately because of bad experiences and setbacks in life, both genders are in the same boat when it comes to feeling that they are not worthy or good enough to actually find someone who will care about them and accept them just the way they are.. But the bottom line is always the same you always attract exactly what you are

For example, I hear reports from people that after a few dates, the discussion moves to who's moving in with whom. When this decision is made, the dynamics automatically change. People want to be loved and feel secure. Even those who don't move in together feel pressured; somehow believing they have to act in a certain way. Every relationship needs to be taken genuinely without the strain of being too serious and uncomfortable. Therefore, allow yourself the freedom to be just who you are and let yourselves get to know each other instead of pretending to always be someone else. There are so many people who think they have to prove themselves to others and act differently than they normally would around friends and family. You may even be focused on a certain type of person and then expect them to be similar to someone you used to know. How fair is that to the new people you meet in life? It would be no different from starting a job and then being expected to behave and even perform the way a former employee did.

Individuals tend to associate their status with their popularity. If they are single, there's no priority involved in a relationship, which may become neglected anyway and therefore has to fight for its survival. That being said, any personal connection whether it is a marriage, friendship or dating all need to be a central focus of attention in a person's life or it will become stagnant, sickly, and slowly die away. I use these terms of comparison to health. Just like we have to keep our bodies nourished and active by giving it the daily attention it needs to be healthy, the longevity of a partnership with someone needs to be addressed as equally as everything else in one's life.

So now if you are ready to have true love in your life, let me ask you this: do you believe it's possible for you? No matter what topic I coach my clients on, if they do not believe in it whether it is a goal or a dream, it can never happen. What you set your intentions and focus on is what you will get out of it, plain and simple. It all begins within you. How are you showing up in the world and what kind of energy are you carrying inside?

At some point, you will have to come to a place of forgiveness and let go of ALL past memories associated with former soul ties, especially if you just started dating or are a newly-wed. Yes, I did say ALL! We are complex human beings; we tend to become emotionally attached to people, places and things. If we continue to keep all memories of failed and damaged relationships in our back pocket we will always be remembering, reliving and becoming expectant from those memories. By referencing the things that did not work out in the past, we are missing the things that can potentially work out for us now.

Here is a list of concerns expressed by my clients that can affect a personal relationship with someone:

- Fear of being trapped or controlled.
- Fear from past abusive (physical, mental, financial) situations.
- Fear of being alone causing people to be needy or co-dependent.
- Fear of being compared to past partners.
- Fear of not measuring up.
- Fear of being taken advantage of again.
- Fear of having to change for someone.
- Fear of commitment based on health issues.
- Fear of ridicule from family or friends.
- Fear of infidelity.
- Fear of not having equal household and financial responsibilities.
- Fear of the change in family dynamics.
- Lack of motivation.
- Low self-esteem.

Given that most of these concerns are fear based, many of my clients have admitted to me that it really does affect their confidence and self-esteem. When it comes to having a successful love life, any kind of struggle may potentially affect a healthy outcome. Once the fears and limiting beliefs are addressed and dealt with, it becomes easier to attract the attention and satisfaction that they long for. This is where shifting your mindset may help individuals turn many of their negative perspectives into positive ones for a potentially healthy and loving relationship.

By establishing honest and trust as well as learning to be a person who is at peace no matter what the outcome may be, you will help to eliminate many fears of the unknown. There should be no apprehension about what the objective of dating really is. For example, do you just want someone to socialize with or are you looking for a life partner? Be upfront and be real. This way, there are no broken hearts and misunderstandings.

So, now that you're ready for love, you know you are not the only one who has had these fears and concerns. You may discover you've got some internal work to do first.

1. If not already addressed, start by clearing out your emotional closet, making room for all the positive and life-enhancing things that you want to welcome in.

2. Go through the steps of forgiveness, which releases all the memories and emotions attached to past relationships.

This will allow you to be focused on what you really want; something new that will compliment and inspire you to bring out the best in you.

Usually at this point, my clients are ready to address the things they have been neglecting that make them who they are. For example, is there something they used to do that made them satisfied and connected to their self? If they have ignored sports, hobbies or interests, there is still a part of them that is unfulfilled. What makes a person so special and unique are the very things that make them happy deep inside.

Now that you have a clear picture of what you really want, you can see that it is possible to even have a goal when it comes to attracting love into your life. When you become focused, your goals become easier to achieve.

Since people cannot be controlled, we have to recognize we can only control and change our own actions and behaviors. For instance, self-esteem is one of the easiest things to change if we can see it that way. Many of my clients quickly understand the connection to first becoming "Love" so that they can attract love into their lives. You see as you go through clearing out your emotional closet, forgiving and releasing old memories both good and bad, your mind becomes void of anything that may have trapped you in the past.

You are empowering yourself to become emotionally clear. Now you are ready to receive and give love that is pure and unaffected from anyone or anything else.

Congratulations!

The following is an exercise I have used with some of my clients who are ready to meet the "Love" of their lives. Here are some sample questions.

Write a letter to either God or the Universe explaining in detail what exactly it is that you are looking for in a partner.

- Be specific about their personality; be detailed about their physical traits (How tall is this person? What is their hair color, length and style?).
- Include their strong points (psychological, intellectual, and physical).
- Talk about your dream life together. Describe what it looks like.
- How old is your ideal partner?
- Am I content and at peace with my life?
- What kind of career does he/she have?
- Do you want children? How many?
- Where do you want to live?

It all begins with you and your choices that will move you in the right direction. If you feel that you would still like to work on some of the things I have discussed above, please feel free to contact me.

Live your life without the limitations of the past or the fear of things that have not yet happened in future relationships. You deserve the best and life wants to give it all to you as well.

Let's work through your limitations now because you really are ready for true love to find you!

What are YOU waiting for?

CHAPTER TWENTY-NINE by Anita Sechesky

Discovering Peace in Your Life

When you've come to a place in your life where you feel like you're trapped or struggling, you may begin to feel constraints or chains that are preventing you from spreading your wings to fly. Many people have expressed these kinds of feelings, not understanding why their lives seem like a losing battle of unknown origins. Limitations are things that can start from early childhood and continue building up until they become walls that literally close you off.

In a sense it may feel like you're trapped in a bird cage. You can see everyone else succeeding, achieving and satisfied in life, but with your own limiting beliefs surrounding you, life may feel hopeless. You know you have greatness within you. You believe there is potential for everyone, but you have adapted the mentality or belief that you're not good enough or you're just not meant to live the way you really want to.

As a Certified Professional Coach, I have helped my clients by guiding them to express where they feel their limitations are stemming from. I ask them powerful questions and reframe situations to help them change their perspectives. Many people have had to face their limitations headfirst to have the courage and determination to achieve a life full of possibilities. My clients discover their own limitations by simply answering my questions or completing assessments.

When my clients express how their dreams look, feel and even "taste," excitement sets in. Once they determine their goals and ambitions, I help them to break them into bite size pieces. When they realistic now. Goals are dreams that develop inside of us before we even have the skills and abilities to achieve them. They then work through a series of various exercises building up their confidence, which usually exposes the most profound limiting mindsets. As they tear away the layers of fears, unforgiveness and pain, trapped emotional energy gets released in the form of tears or jubilation, peace and confidence begins to emerge once again. They realize they are free to set new goals once thought of as unreachable dreams. The things that were once weighing them down emotionally and spiritually are now gone.

Through "The Act of Forgiveness," I have mentored many people who have had the most profound breakthroughs. Realistically, we cannot change anyone; we can only change ourselves. Disappointments happen, but they don't need to be the focus of a life seeking joy and fulfillment. Moving forward they realized situations once perceived as negative experiences may not have been as harsh.

You see, when living a life with a limiting mindset, everything around you becomes a misrepresentation of what your life can be. You may feel small or you're in a losing battle with life. Learning to shift your perspectives with a trained coach will help you to feel validated and heal so much quicker than struggling for years on your own. What you carry around inside of you emotionally is what you will attract into your life. You'll only be focused on what you feel.

Here are some key questions about limiting mindsets and perceptions in life:

Limitations Questionnaire

1. Q – Have you ever experienced poor treatment in your life by others?
   A – You may have a baggage of limitations.

2. Q – Do you feel like you're spinning in circles and not going anywhere?
   A – You have no clear direction. More than likely you have a limitation in your life preventing you from succeeding.

3. Q – Do you feel like you're like that bird in the cage?
   A – Your limitations are an invisible cage. Your wings are meant to fly.

4. Q – What kind of environment are you subjecting yourself to?
   A – This could include your exposure to destructive or harsh entertainment (movies, books, and video games), abusive or neglectful relationships, substance abuse, toxic work environments or adverse living conditions.

5. Q – What is your self talk like?
   A – Allowing negative self talk from yourself or others is destructive to self!

6. Q – How do you show up in the world?
   A – Presentation is key to success. Don't limit yourself. Take the extra time that's needed to pull your look together.

7. Q – Do have a hard time forgiving others?
   A – Holding on to resentment and anger will only cause you harm by blockages in your personal perceptions.

Many people have learned that certain lifestyle exposures will directly affect their attitudes, emotions or health. Many people are still afraid of stepping out of their comfort zone, staying trapped by that invisible bird cage.

Life Without Limitations Questionnaire

1. Q – Are you confident enough to achieve success without permission?

   A – Living without limitations does not require consent from others.

2. Q – Do you have a dream?

   A – You have been given a gift from your Creator that's all yours.

3. Q – Can you see your dream happen?

   A – When you envision your dreams come to life, you create your realities.

4. Q – Do you have goals hidden inside that direct your steps?

   A – Clear, concise and achievable goals equal success.

5. Q – Do you speak positively?

   A – Positive self talk and reinforcement increase self-esteem and confidence.

6. Q – Do you step out of your comfort zone?

   A – You can't show up in life if you don't step out.

7. Q – How does it feel when you forgive others?

   A – Forgiving others releases personal bondages and limiting beliefs about life and people in general. Forgiveness heals!

Everyone around us who has achieved success in their lives have learned at some point that they can do it. They didn't wait for permission to be the best that they can be. They didn't let their fear of failure stop them. In fact, it is common knowledge that many people who do succeed have failed many times and learned from their own mistakes, or the mistakes of others.

I allow my clients to express their concerns and help them to understand where their limitations or despair are coming from. Coaches set goals that are entirely client focused and accountable to them. With this type of professional relationship, clients explore their own paths in life and what speed they want to move forward.

People facing extreme limitations may have a great need for emotional release when trapped by their own or others' limiting beliefs. A number of them have dealt with all kinds of negative life experiences, such as the loss of a loved one, lost finances, job termination, health setbacks, divorce, physical, verbal or mental abuse, and even racial limitations. I have observed how this affects their self-worth and confidence. When they become more focused, they learn how to heal and maintain balance in their lives to be able to be the best for their loved ones.

The Art of Forgiveness!

1. Consider adapting "The Art of Forgiveness" into your life. This is done by setting time aside to reflect on life events that resulted in unpleasant and negative unresolved feelings. This is one of the "Biggest" doors to opening limitations in life. Everything will be affected by those negative feelings—your choices, attitudes, and your health—if you let them fester for too long. They may possibly show up as different forms of stress or anxiety, leading to more serious health conditions.

2. You have to understand and accept that Forgiveness is needed, as you cannot change the past or even other people. You can only change yourself. Decide to recall and write down the names of these people who have hurt you or let you down.

3. When you have listed as many that come to your mind, it doesn't matter how far back you go. Start saying, "I forgive... I now release all of the pain, disappointment and heartache they have caused me."

4. Once you have done this with the entire list, you may find yourself emotionally released quickly. No one should ever have power over you to that extent unless you allow it. Words and things done in the past are in the past. Words have power and negative word cycles can be broken and replaced with positive reinforcement. We cannot change the past but we can choose to make a better future, free of pain.

5. Now that you have done this, it is time for you to recognize how amazing and POWERFUL you really are! You are the only one who can make a difference in your life. Remove your limitations. You get to choose. Choose Love!

If anything that I have shared in this chapter resonates with you, PLEASE contact me. I believe that each one of you has "Greatness" within! Don't let labels, failures, lack, or your own limiting beliefs separate you from the joy, happiness, peace, fulfillment and satisfaction that God and the Universe want to bless you with.

You are valued and greatly appreciated. It's time to spread your wings and fly without limitations. Ready! Set! GO!!

CONCLUSION

Thank you for reading our book. It is my hope that you have been enlightened with the essence of what peace really means to the human spirit. *"#Peace – A New Perspective of Hope"* is a highly sought after book and successful because all thirty of my co-authors including myself share how our own peaceful ways of recreating our lives with forgiveness and acceptance have given us a life full of unlimited possibilities. By choosing to have an attitude of love and peace, it has helped us to find balance in our daily lives.

My intention with this anthology was to encourage you to reassess your own life and how you may have allowed past experiences to affect the life you are living today. With so many peaceful and empowering perspectives revealed in this book, it would be a blessing to see how we can change the world with just a little more love, peace, and unity, one soul at a time. I encourage you to give up the things that have hurt you or held you back in life. Allow yourself the permission and let go of your own personal limitations as you continue to ponder the wisdom and life experiences of all our contributions. We have all willingly permitted you into our world regardless of how painful and damaged our emotions have been through various situations that eventually led us to find the peace we all sought after.

The significance that is within our beautiful book is everlasting. Just like gold never loses its value, the many perspectives of what peace means to us is tenderly poured into each chapter. This kind of insight alone is immense and worthy of examination and application in one's daily life.

Now, my question to you is: "Do you have a vision for a beautiful book of your own? Do you want to inspire, motivate, and encourage others? Do you feel you can help people to live a life without limiting beliefs? Have you gone through something that is incredible and know that others need to hear your story?" I would be honored to guide and coach you into compiling and writing your own life changing anthology if you are a visionary that believes in yourself but just need the professional support and guidance to pull it all together. What are you waiting for? Contact me and let's discuss what your next steps would be to become one of LWL PUBLISHING HOUSE's international VIP Compilers.

I have successfully managed, coached, and organized 5 groups of international co-authors in the last three years, and now have published this fifth anthology! That's approximately 200 people from around the world who are now recognized as leaders and experts among their peers!

I would love to help you organize and manage your book project as it is also considered a wise entrepreneurial step to build your business through a book.

As the Founder and Publisher of LWL PUBLISHING HOUSE, I have supported and mentored other clients successfully and would love to help you become a Best-Selling author as well.

I have learned so much about people and what makes them inspired and motivated from over ten years of specialized experience as a Registered Nurse in the health care field, as well as my extensive training to become a Level 3 – Advanced Certified Life Coach, Marketing and Media Diva, NLP Practitioner, Law of Attraction Wealth Practitioner, LWL Conference/workshop host and trainer, and now a Best-Seller Publisher. People cope not just effectively but successfully, just by having an organized system that brings balance with positive results! There really is a secret to helping others succeed just for you! I want to show you how as my VIP client.

I understand it's not always easy to keep things running smoothly, whether it relates to your business, personal goals and obligations, while still building the life of your dreams. I understand the frustrations, tears, and stress. I want to assist you in making your dreams and goals a reality as a published author and I want to show you how to do it as quickly as possible, as you live your life with a passion and purpose, while earning a financial BONUS on the day of book launch, just for bringing your book to life. Let's get started. Connect with me and let me coach you from the introduction to the publication of your book!

Together we will develop a "Master Plan template for your Publishing success" and along the way we just may be eliminating any kind of "Limiting Beliefs" that's been robbing you from achieving success. You may even be surprised at what you discover. Your passion is always where your strength lies. My passion is all about bringing your passion to life in print without limitations!

To begin the exciting journey as a VIP Compiler™ with me on your own anthology book, or to learn more about becoming a co-author with LWL PUBLISHING HOUSE in any one of our multiple anthologies, *Co-authoring opportunities limited per book.

Please visit our Facebook page "LWL PUBLISHING HOUSE", You can visit our website: www.lwlpublishinghouse.com

or email: lwlclienthelp@gmail.com.

Currently, we are looking for co-authors for all of our #Hashtag books in the series and more...

#Hope – A New Way to Think

#Joy – The Emotion to Embrace

#Success - Found within Me

Join my Private Facebook group: LIVING WITHOUT LIMITATIONS LIFESTYLE – With exclusive prizes, co-authoring opportunities and Random Contests with FREE Publishing opportunities. *Empowerment Webinar classes and more - http://bit.ly/1TlsTSm

Book Facebook Fan page: http://bit.ly/211XffM

Facebook: s://www.facebook.com/AnitaSechesky/

Email: lwlclienthelp@gmail.com

YouTube Channel: http://bit.ly/1VEGHew

Website: www.anitasechesky.com

LinkedIn: https://ca.linkedin.com/in/asechesky

Twitter: https://twitter.com/nursie4u

Anita Sechesky

Best-Seller Publisher, Book Writing Coach, Registered Nurse, Certified Professional Coach, NLP and LOA Wealth Practitioner, multiple International Best-Selling Author, Workshop Facilitator, Conference Host, Founder and CEO of Anita Sechesky - Living Without Limitations Inc., Founder and Publisher of LWL PUBLISHING HOUSE.

Available on all Amazon sites.
http://amzn.to/1SzkTuD

Available on all Amazon sites.
http://amzn.to/1TcNMMR

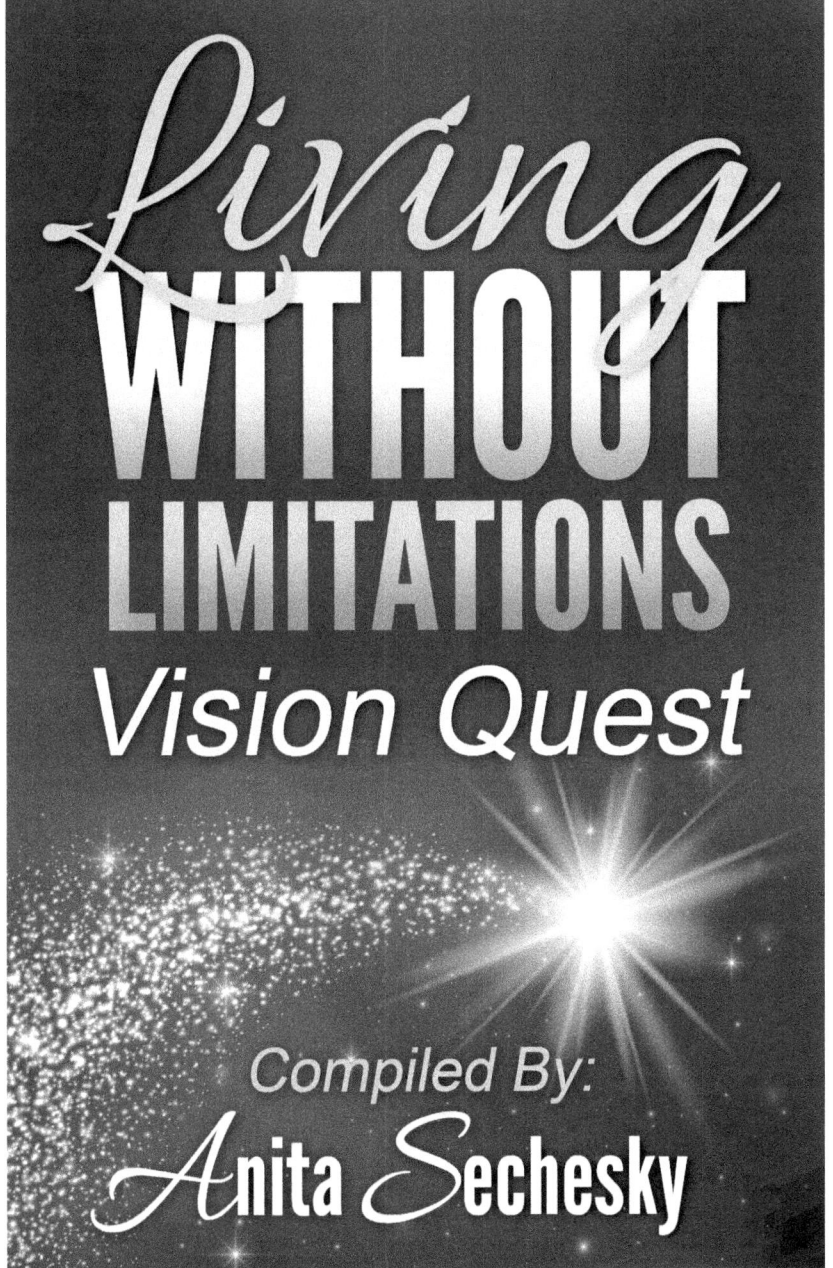

www.ingramcontent.com/pod-product-compliance
Lightning Source LLC
Chambersburg PA
CBHW070610300426
44113CB00010B/1478